ANGELS: WINGED WHISPERS

True Stories from Angel Experts
around the World

Edited by Sophia Fairchild

FOREWORD BY FLAVIA KATE PETERS

SOUL WINGS® PRESS
Sydney, Australia
Laguna Beach, CA, USA

Published by Soul Wings® Press
Publishing for the Soul®
www.SoulWingsPress.com

Editorial Supervision by Sophia Fairchild
Book Design by Fiona Raven

Library of Congress Cataloging-in-Publication data
Angels : winged whispers , true stories from angel experts around the world / edited by Sophia Fairchild ; foreword by Flavia Kate Peters.
p. cm.
ISBN 978-0-9845-9301-9
1. Angels. 2. Spirituality. 3. Spirituality—Anecdotes. 4. Self-actualization (Psychology)—Problems, exercises, etc. I. Fairchild, Sophia. II. Peters, Flavia Kate. III. Title.
BL477 .A54 2011   291.2/15 –dc22   2010918890
Digital ISBN: 978-0-9845-9304-0

First Printing April 2011
Printed in the United States of America

Published by Soul Wings® Press
Publishing for the Soul®
668 N Coast Hwy, Suite 234
Laguna Beach, CA 92651, USA
125 Oxford Street, Suite 125
Bondi Junction NSW 2022 Australia
www.SoulWingsPress.com

"The magical pages of *Angels: Winged Whispers* take us through what some may deem as extraordinary stories of people who have had encounters with angels. We are introduced to various methods of working with the angels, such as sacred ceremony, working with crystals, receiving direct messages and noticing signs. Within each chapter is a wealth of delight as the writers share their own unique stories and teachings with us, so that we too may have our own very real connection with angels. So feast your eyes on this treasury of insights, stories, teachings and messages, and awaken to the miracles in your life."

—FLAVIA KATE PETERS, Author, Speaker, Singer,
Angel Therapist® and Faery Facilitator
www.angel-lights.co.uk

"I was deeply touched and moved by the stories included in this collection. They are refreshingly honest, full of insight and prove that although our experiences may vary, we are all the same in our desire to feel more peace and love. If you want to be inspired, uplifted and reminded that you are never alone on this journey called life, then I highly recommend you read this book!"

—ANNA TAYLOR, Recording Artist, Singer – Songwriter,
Angel Therapist® and Theta Healing Practitioner®
www.anna-taylor.co.uk and www.annataylormusic.com

"Although written by individual authors, these vibrant stories share a communal message that illuminates the truth of how loved, protected and supported all of us truly are. This book affectionately invites the reader to notice the abundance of Divine Guidance that surrounds us constantly, lovingly reminding us that this guidance might arrive in the form of a cat, a butterfly, a stranger or an angel."

—MARK MEZADOURIAN, Angelic Ambassador
of Courses, Workshops and Readings
www.markmezadourian.com

"*Angels: Winged Whispers* is a book about real people and real life stories that can be related to on so many levels of life. The insight given through the authors' experiences are bound to bring readers the realization that they too have received signs from "heaven" (angels, fairies and even deceased loved ones). This book is filled with messages of wonder, inspiration and speaks to your heart at a soul level."

—CINDY EYLER, Author of "Dead People in My Life."
Internationally known Spiritual and Transformational Journey Leader,
and Founder of Light Activation Healing System®
www.HealingYourSoul.com and www.LightActivation.com

This book is dedicated
with eternal gratitude to
the angels
and to lightworkers
everywhere.

Contents

Foreword

Angels.
Angels??!

Can they *really* help us?

Are they really able to assist us with every aspect of our lives, and even bestow miracles upon us?

How could this be so?

Sure, I've heard of Archangel Gabriel bringing a message to the shepherds about a Messiah being born, but why would an angel come to me?

I'm just an ordinary person. Things like that wouldn't happen to me!!

Would they?

Yes they would!

We are all equal in the eyes of the Creator and also in the eyes of the angels. This means that each and every one of us deserves love, attention and *miracles* to happen in our lives.

During these times of huge changes, more and more people are experiencing 'angel encounters' as angels flock to our planet, making themselves readily available to everyone who calls upon them. The angels' mission is to heal us from our challenges and to instill peace and love into our hearts, so that we may focus on our own life purpose. The angels are always in the background waiting patiently for us to ask for advice and guidance, so that they can gently and lovingly lead us in the right direction.

We can call as many angels into our life as we'd like, and the more we think about them, the more angels will surround us. The angels' energy lifts us greatly, especially when we truly feel their loving presence.

There are absolutely no limits to the ways angels can assist us. They can help us with relationships, careers, finances and any other challenge that may be troubling us. They urge us to listen to and connect with them, and will often try to contact us directly, or perhaps lead us to someone who can help us to become more aware of their presence, or guide us to a certain book . . . and it is by no mistake that you are reading these words today.

The magical pages of *Angels: Winged Whispers* take us through what some may deem as *extraordinary* stories of people who have had encounters with angels, of how the angels have sent messages to these ordinary people in the form of animals or deceased loved ones, or through words, thoughts and visions, to save or transform their lives in some way.

Within each chapter is a wealth of delight as the writers share their own unique stories and teachings with us, so that we too may have our own very *real* connection with angels.

As the reader, we are introduced to various methods of working with the angels, such as sacred ceremony, working with crystals, receiving direct messages and noticing signs. We are given clear reminders to call upon the angels for comfort in times of need, and of bereavement, bridging Heaven and Earth.

We are also introduced to working with those magical manifestors, the faeries (Nature's Angels), and how we may connect with and be at one with the natural world of magic that is within and all around us.

Now is the time for us to awaken to the gifts that we have denied ourselves for so long. The angels are waiting . . .

So feast your eyes on this treasury of insights, stories, teachings and messages, and awaken to the miracles in your life. The more you notice them, the more they will happen.

May you always walk with angels . . .

FLAVIA KATE PETERS
Newbury, Berkshire
United Kingdom

Introduction

When I was a small child, I found myself in a children's home, the kind of place where orphaned children were offered food, shelter and charity, but little love. Not wanting to live in such a world, I made the solemn decision to hide under my bed in the long, drafty dormitory and hold my breath until I went to heaven. At the time, this seemed my only escape from what seemed like a loveless world.

But then an angel came to me and wrapped me in the warmth of her wings. She told me not to give up. She said that I would grow up to love a child of my own some day and that I would live a long life, filled with wonderful adventures! And so, from that moment forward, I knew I was no longer alone and have felt the angels' reassuring presence with me ever since.

Each one of us has guardian angels beside us throughout our entire lifetime. They are here to protect and help us in many ways, specifically to find peace in our hearts. In fact, a recent survey shows that more than half the people in America believe they have been protected from harm by a guardian angel. The word *angel* means "messenger of God." All angels, including Nature Angels, are overseen by Archangels who are "the greatest messengers of God," *Arch* meaning "the greatest" or "first."

Because Archangels are egoless and have no physical form, they are limitless beings, able to assist an unlimited number of people simultaneously. We should never be afraid to ask for their support, thinking we're depriving others of their aid, because they can be with everyone who calls for their help in any given moment.

Angels love everyone equally and unconditionally and offer their assistance to each of us regardless of who we are. This means that we don't need to be especially 'chosen' or to have a particular set of religious beliefs for the angels to grace us with their presence. Angels are in fact nondenominational and have appeared in all the world's religions throughout recorded history as God's intercessors here on earth. They are here, not to be worshipped, but to help replace all of our fears with love.

Because each of us is born with free will, the angels cannot intervene on our behalf unless they've been given permission to do so. Therefore we must ask for their assistance before they're able to help us. It doesn't matter how we ask; all that matters is that we make our request. The angels know how best to help us, and their assistance may come in surprising ways. Angels are all around us at all times, and no request is too big or too small.

It is not necessary to be able to see an angel to receive their loving support. When angels come to us during a time of need, they will appear in a form that we can best understand. Visitations may occur in dreams or visions. Angelic assistance may also come in the form of a Nature Angel, or another human being who appears out of nowhere to offer unexpected support.

Many people perceive the angels' presence as a warm and comforting sensation, perhaps associated with tingling and an apparent change in air pressure. Others who are more visually sensitive perceive the angels' sparkling energy field as flashes of colored light. Some report receiving messages through repeated symbols. Many will experience events characterized by synchronicity or profound coincidence. Others perceive heavenly music or clearly audible messages directly from their angels.

All of the above may be classified as 'whispers from the angels,' their sincere attempts to communicate with us in a form we can best comprehend. And during our lifetime, each one of us will discover our own unique way of interacting with the angelic realm.

The angels are constantly whispering guidance to us through our everyday experiences – our vision, hearing, thoughts, feelings and dreams – patiently repeating their messages until we are able to understand their loving communication. We need not strain or try to force this process. Our task is to remain receptive, allowing these angelic whispers to reach us through our natural sensory perception and day to day activities.

Some people may feel they are unworthy to hear the loving whispers of the angels. However, the more we relax and allow the angels to help us, the more benefit we bring to the world around us. Angelic guidance is not only designed to help us all find peace in our hearts, but is always intended with love.

As you will discover through the pages of this book, each Angel Expert brings to their professional practice a unique approach. Some combine working with the angels with dreams and crystals, while others work with Mediumship, animals or the Nature Angels. Each brings years of expertise gathered from a variety of specialized fields to their current practice. All are inspired in their daily life by the loving presence of angels. The rich diversity of personal experiences they share here is truly a precious gift. Cherish their wisdom and enjoy!

By sharing their stories, the authors of this book wish to inspire you to explore new approaches and techniques that will help you and your clients experience the deep wisdom and loving power of the angelic realm to comfort, uplift and heal every aspect of your life!

May your journey through *Angels: Winged Whispers* help you to more clearly perceive the persistent nudges and whispered messages offered by your Guardian Angels, the Archangels, Animals and Faeries, all awaiting your discovery!

SOPHIA FAIRCHILD
Sydney, Australia

WENDY GABRIEL

Wisconsin, USA

WENDY GABRIEL is an Angel Therapy Practitioner®, Medium, and professional spiritual teacher, trained and certified by Dr. Doreen Virtue.

She currently resides in Wisconsin, and she is on track to become a Doctor of Oriental Medicine in 2015.

She plans to specialize in palliative care.

Contact Wendy at www.angelgalwendy.com

The Butterfly Keeper

WENDY GABRIEL

*Whenever you send up a prayer for assistance, the Universe always responds.
Sometimes the healing and assistance you receive may not be what you requested;
it is, however, always what you need.*

$\mathcal{M}$y nose is in a book, and I am deep in the world of the body – endocrine system, reproduction, brain chemistry – when the buzz of my cell phone breaks my concentration. It's my 10-year-old daughter Emily, calling me at college to let me know she's home from school. I am a pre-med student, and I spend an extraordinary amount of time on campus. Normally, Emily just checks in quickly and then lets me return to my world of biology. But today's call is different. She tells me she's harboring a fugitive in our kitchen – a butterfly, rescued as she performed bus duty an hour ago. It's strictly against the rules to touch bugs found on school grounds, Emily confesses. But she saw the butterfly resting on the blacktop and was shocked to see one of her classmates deliberately roll over it with his bicycle.

"I took it and hid it from the teacher, even though I wasn't supposed to!" she reports breathlessly, a little shocked by her brazen violation of the rules. Emily's normally a very by-the-book fifth grader. "I snuck it home under my shirt because I didn't want anything else to happen to it! I have it here now."

"Mom, Emily brought a bug into the kitchen!" I hear my 12-year-old son Joe call in the background. He's full of mischief and takes every opportunity to tease his sister mercilessly.

"Shut *up*, Joe!" she orders, hand over the mouthpiece of the phone. Then she's back with me. "I'm making it a plate of sugar water, in case it's hungry. I brought it some dandelion flowers from the yard. What else do you think it needs?"

"Well, maybe it just left its cocoon," I say wisely, full of knowledge about the world of bugs and biology and everything else a parent needs to know. "You know, butterflies need time to let their wings dry. They can't fly while their wings are wet. They just sort of sit around in the sun – maybe that's why the butterfly was on the ground.

"Just let it sit for a bit," I advise, "and let's see what happens."

When I get home from class a few hours later, I see the truth of the situation: Emily's rescued butterfly is not at the beginning of its life, but at the end. It's horribly injured: the bottom part of its left wing is missing; its right wing is badly torn; a couple legs are bent at impossible angles. It rests on a white kitchen towel, its legs crumpled beneath it like the wilting petals of dandelion blooms that Emily had placed carefully around it. The small saucer of sugar water is untouched.

"Emily, I'm so sorry," I tell her gently. "I don't think your butterfly is going to make it."

Joe, who's rummaging around in the refrigerator, stops his endless foraging to make a mock gasping sound, then break into fake sobs. I look away from Emily and her charge long enough to cast him a dirty look. When I see Emily again, her face is contorted. She's taking every ounce of self-control not to break down. I send Joe out of the kitchen just in time. Emily's chest heaves and she bursts into tears, devastated.

I watch her, detached but concerned. I believe everything happens for a reason. There must be a lesson here . . . I wonder why this tiny creature has been sent into our lives.

"I don't want it to die!" Emily says, gasping through her tears. "Why are people so mean? Why did that boy run it over? Why did it have to be right there, right at that time, when there are so many other places to be? It could have been anywhere, anywhere in the great big sky!"

I just nod my head in agreement and stroke my daughter's beautiful long hair. The illusion of mommy-wisdom has vanished, and I have no words, no wisdom for her. This beautiful creature will die too soon.

Then, I think of a beautiful *person* who will be taken too soon – Marsha, Joe and Emily's aunt. I had divorced her brother nearly five years earlier, but Marsha remains a beloved friend to me, an adopted sister that I love deeply. She fought and defeated breast cancer a decade ago; but now, it's returned, and this time, it's metastasized, spread to her spine. "It's not a matter of *if* it'll kill me," she told me grimly last May, "but *when*."

At first, Marsha fought the new cancer – rounds of chemo, radiation, fistfuls of meds. But that was 12 months ago. Today, Marsha is growing tired of fighting. Soon, her light will go the way of this butterfly's spirit.

When Marsha broke the news to me, I was devastated. How could I tell my children that their beloved aunt was dying? I did the only thing I knew – I took my grief to God. In prayer, I pleaded with God for a miracle. I begged the Universe to spare her life, to heal her miraculously and grant her many more years on earth. Failing that, I prayed that God would ease her transition, blunt her pain, and then give me the words to help Joe and Emily when the time came. I prayed to God to send angels to bring Marsha and my children comfort. And I prayed that God might give my children the tools to cope with this loss and to help them understand that, even in death, relationships can go on.

As I remember these things, I suddenly *know* – I know why Emily saw the butterfly get run over this afternoon. I know why she took it upon herself to covertly snatch it up and sneak it home, against school rules. And I know why she sobs now, even if she doesn't really understand. Both Joe and Emily have always been tremendously intuitive. They've been told that Aunt Marsha is sick; they have not been told she's dying. Now, Emily knows. She knows without *knowing*. She feels the pain and loss without knowing specifically *why*.

But *I* know why she suffers. And now tears are in *my* eyes, as well. I search for the right words. I know I am smoothing a path for a greater loss ahead. I send a silent prayer out to my guardian angel. *Help me find the words*. I am silent a moment, wiping tears away with the back of my hand. And then I feel the comfort of my guardian angel by my side, a distinctive fullness in my heart that fills me with peace.

Just speak from your heart, the angel replies. I nod and exhale slowly.

"All things pass," I tell Emily (and myself.) "The spirit that makes this butterfly unique and special will transition from the physical to the spirit. But it will still be with us, always with us, part of all that is."

I'm not sure Emily's even listening. She's shaking her head, squeezing her eyes now, willing the grief out of her body. Fat tears slide down her freckled cheeks, onto the towel below. I watch as the butterfly struggles to lift a spindly leg, resting it beside her finger. It's barely touching her, but it is contact. Emily stops crying for a moment, looking at the butterfly with concern and wonder beneath wet lashes. The butterfly's wings are dark, speckled with tan on the edges. The part of the hind wing that remains reveals brilliant spots of blue, the color of the clearest skies. Its antennae are long and exquisitely ornate, with feathered bulbs at the end. Its long proboscis is curled tight against its face. I wonder if it knows that my daughter grieves for it. I hope it knows. I wonder if Marsha knows. I hope she does.

"Send it love," I advise Emily. "Try to feel gratitude in your heart for its presence in your life. You've only known it for a little while, but it's brought you so many gifts."

"But why am I so freaked out about a stupid bug?" she wails, tears starting again.

"That's what I'm wondering," Joe calls from the other room.

"It's just a freakin' bug!" she adds, ashamed. "It's not like it's my aunt!"

My stomach clenches involuntarily at her words. This child truly has no idea how very psychic she is . . .

"You don't cry every time you step on an ant, do you?" Joe adds.

"Joe," I admonish, but my words falter. I don't know what else to say.

I know why she's crying.

The really touching thing about Marsha is that *she* would understand Emily's grief over this insect, even without a larger life-or-death context. Marsha is such a lover of nature, she'd cry over this tiny creature's suffering in a heartbeat. Her sweet, gentle spirit is famous among her friends and family. As a girl, the story goes, she helped her father in the garden. Her job was to thin the newly planted sprouts, making room in the rows for the plants to grow. After a while, her father noticed her pulling out all of the big plants, but leaving the runts in the dirt. "I just thought they needed a little help!" she explained, raising her eyebrows at the memory. "They weren't doing as well as the others, probably because those bigger plants were stealing all the sunlight!"

That's Marsha, in a nutshell – she stands up for the underdog, she protects the weak, and she passionately loves animals and people. If ever there was an angel on earth, it's her.

My thoughts turn from Marsha back to my children. It's now time for bed. Emily reluctantly takes a photograph of her winged friend with her digital camera and tells it goodnight. She knows it will not be alive in the morning. I tuck her in and hold her as she cries. I tell her she is never wrong for feeling grief – it means that her heart is open, that she *can* love. I tell her to be glad for *everyone* in her life that she loves. When she falls asleep, her blue satin pillowcase is stained with tears.

When I tuck Joe in, he looks at me with eyes so huge and brown, they're almost bovine. I meet his gaze and tell him silently that his beloved aunt is going to die soon. I'm not allowed to say the words aloud. Marsha is my ex-husband's sister; he's decided it's best to not burden the kids with the seriousness of the situation until . . .

Answered Prayer

Your angels assure you that your prayers have been heard and answered.

The answers to your prayers are all around you. Notice the synchronicities, dreams, signs and messages that are appearing in your life. Every prayer is always answered. Be open to receiving angelic guidance and assistance in surprising ways.

until . . . well, until she's in the last few weeks of her life. I understand my ex's thinking. I really do. His family, my family – none of us have ever handled death or grief very well. It's something to be stoic about, something to get over. Emotions are messy, irrational things. Nothing can be done.

But as Joe looks at me with serious eyes, I know he knows, as well. The unspoken words between us are thick and sad, and I can tell he doesn't want to believe any of it. He's going into seventh grade soon. He wants to be a man. He wants to shave and have a girlfriend and drive a Corvette. He doesn't want to believe in unspoken knowing; he doesn't want to feel this grief, thick in his heart. He doesn't want to know about death or angels or God or what, if anything, comes next. He wants to be like his dad, to be stoic, to move on. I hug him hard and press my cheek against his, a stolen moment of affection from my normally hands-off boy. "I *love* you," I tell him softly. And I mean it.

The chill of evening comes and I can hear the chorus of frogs outside, a spring-time symphony of life playing out in the pond outside my back door. On my kitchen table, the butterfly's wings are spread flat now, making tiny, involuntary jerking motions. I want the poor thing to be out of pain. Its suffering makes no sense to me, and I'm grateful that Emily's in bed and cannot see this now. I pray that its wing movements mean that it's slipped from consciousness and is now in the Dreamtime, where the wind slides beneath its wings and it's free to soar into the sun.

I think of Marsha, away now in California, in the care and comfort of her family. *Does she know?* I wonder. *Does she know how much she is loved? Could she ever possibly* really *understand?* The answer, of course, is no. If I called her and told her so, she'd just say, "Oh," and laugh a little, then change the subject. Because Marsha's always been most at home *giving* others love and attention; the receiving end makes her squirm. I ache to think of the pain she suffers now. I want her to soar like the butterfly, her spirit unbound, free from time and gravity and earth and pain. And yet, I want her here, with me, now.

I offer up a one-word prayer to Heaven, a simple sigh of my mind: *God . . .* There's no need to finish the thought; I cannot finish. The love that flows through all, the eternal power of everything . . . well, "He/She/It" knows the rest. I look at the butterfly and send it a wave of love from my heart. "Thank you," I say aloud, softly. "Thank you."

It gently sinks into the towel and is still.

That night, I cannot sleep. The image of that butterfly burns my mind. As my thoughts drift, I remember something I learned in my first college biology class. When a caterpillar enters its cocoon, it essentially dies. In my mind's eye, I can see the caterpillar's body dissolving into a gelatinous mass. Then I envision special-ized cells called "imaginal cells" sparking to life, building a new body. As I drift in and out of sleep, I imagine that these imaginal cells are building the body of a butterfly. Proteins assemble, organs are built, wings take shape, and when it is time, my dream butterfly nudges forth from its cocoon into its new existence. *That must be what death is like,* I think hazily. *I wonder if the caterpillar is ever afraid when it goes into its cocoon. I wonder if the butterfly ever mourns what it left behind . . .*

A few months later, there is more loss to mourn. Cosmo, our silky black housecat, has fallen suddenly ill. Although he's 14 years old, he's always been the picture of health. But overnight, he's gone from chasing dogs and lounging in sunbeams to a curled mass of fur on the end of the bed. He refuses to eat or drink, and when he stands, he limps painfully. He is so weak, he cannot even meow. A visit to the veterinarian reveals the unthinkable – his spleen has ruptured. We bring Cosmo home to die.

We place Cosmo in his favorite spot at the foot of Joe's bed, and Emily and I place our hands over Cosmo to send him reiki. We're both perplexed, stunned with disbelief that our furry friend could be so healthy one day and at death's doorstep the next. Again, Emily is inconsolable. I watch her weep, my heart aching for her; my heart aching for Cosmo. And silently I ask the angels, *Why? Why is this happening? Why take Cosmo now?* I do not receive an answer. I can only hear Cosmo's purring, thick and deep, and feel his smooth fur beneath my fingertips. I can only pet my daughter's hair as she lies beside him, crying.

But that night, I dream. Beings of light are laying a path, bit by bit. Each stone goes into place with great effort, but once the stones are set, they are strong and true. The labor is long and difficult, but the path leads to a beautiful place. I cannot see the destination, but I can *feel* it; it is filled with great love. When I awaken, blinking in the early-morning sunlight, I am filled with peace and comfort, and I know that Cosmo's sacrifice, his quick departure from this earth, is but another step that will prepare both Emily and Joe's hearts for Marsha's death.

I am not surprised to discover that Cosmo died peacefully during the night. We bury him beneath a fragrant flower bush in the backyard. That night, the kids and I sit and look at Cosmo's kitten photos, laughing through our tears at the silly, spiky-haired kitty who loved drinking water from the fish tank, letting his tail swirl in the water as he pawed at the fish. I find myself telling Emily and Joe what I believe about death, telling them truths that I've learned during my years as a medium and an Angel Therapy Practitioner. As I speak the words, I know the angels are speaking through me.

Death is the end of this lifetime on earth, but it's also a birth of sorts. It's the beginning of a new life, elsewhere. The veil between our world and the next is very thin. Those who are lost to us here can always be reached, communicated with. Although they are not in flesh, they are still with us, sending us love, compassion; serving as our companions. We have only to acknowledge their existence to really start to feel their company.

Joe rolls his eyes, stands up and leaves. But Emily sits in front of the photo album, her eyes unfocused. I know in my heart that as painful as these last few months have been, they have been God's way of strengthening her heart, of helping her get used to the idea of loss. It's strange to imagine that all of this pain could be the answer to a prayer, but intuitively, I know it is so. While it's true that I didn't get the miracle I'd prayed for – Marsha is still dying – the Universe did provide my kids with some tools to help withstand her departure.

And for that, I will always be grateful.

I have learned that once a loved one crosses, our relationship with him or her is far from over. The morning after my beloved grandmother, Tula, crossed, I could *feel* her energy in my home. She had never been well enough to visit me at my home in the Midwest, but once she was in spirit, she was like an excited child finally getting to take a long-awaited trip. She stayed by my side all day long, running a non-stop commentary in my head.

Oh! Look at how big those kids are! Those were the first words I heard in my head as Joey and Emily, then ages 3 and 1, came tumbling from their bedrooms and into my bed in the morning. *And so beautiful! Now, what will they eat for breakfast?*

It was amazing! Just hours earlier, I had gotten the phone call that she had died. Now, she was the same Gramie Tula she had always been – chatty, concerned about her family, and now, focused on feeding them! I laughed with joy as I realized that even though her transition was very difficult and sad, now she was just fine! She had longed to be with her great-grandchildren all the time. Now, she was able to live that dream. After we fed the kids (pancakes and sausage – Gramie's choice!), Gramie Tula and I sat together on the porch swing in the backyard and watched the kids play on the swing set. I could *feel* her warmth beside me, *feel* her pressure against my leg, *hear* her voice in my head. I *knew* she was truly beside me.

As the afternoon progressed, Gramie Tula thanked me for my prayers and all of the energy work I had done on her as she prepared to transition from lung cancer. During the last few weeks of her life, she had been unable to communicate with anyone in the three-dimensional realm. But I had maintained a vigil of prayers and love, sending reiki to soothe her spirit and ease her transition. I had also prayed that Archangel Azrael assist her and the rest of our family. She said that she felt every bit of love, felt every prayer, saw every angel that I asked to join her. It was a beautiful confirmation that the work that I did to help her really did make a difference.

Working with Loved Ones who Transition
My experience with Gramie Tula, both immediately after her death and in the years since, has strengthened my belief in two important things: the power of helping someone transition, and our ability to continue our relationships with our loved ones, even after death.

Even if you are unable to physically be with a loved one during the time leading up to her transition, your prayers, love, and energy are all deeply felt by her on many different levels. If the dying person is comatose, some are able to connect with their loved ones during meditation and get a sense of unfinished business that the loved one wishes to complete. Transcribing channeled messages that the loved one gives you, performing small acts of kindness as instructed by your loved one, or even praying for the loved one's family members are all acts of service that can help ease the transition from life to death.

Archangel Azrael can assist those who are struggling with grief or loss, as well. Azrael has the rather dramatic moniker, "The Angel of Death," but in truth, he's happy to help anyone through transitions of all sorts. All you have to do is ask him for help. It's as easy as praying, "Archangel Azrael, please bring comfort and peace to my loved one as she prepares for her death. Please ease her suffering, and smooth her transition. Please also ease the pain of her loved ones who are left behind. Thank you." Angels can be anywhere and everywhere, all at once; they can help as many people as they need to. You need not ever worry about "bother-ing" Archangel Azrael or any other angel, for that matter.

Once your loved one has passed, look for signs that he or she is near. You may get a clear sign, such as a white feather or a colorful flower left in a random place. Many people have stories about finding 'pennies from heaven' left by their loved ones. You may receive messages from your loved one through your psychic channels – seeing visions, experiencing a sudden knowing, experiencing a physical touch or smell. Or you may actually 'hear' your loved one's voice in your head, as I did.

While some folks can hear the voices of the departed as clearly as if their loved ones were standing behind them, speaking, my clairaudience comes in a different way. I 'heard' my grandmother's voice the way that I 'hear' a strain of music from a favorite song when I remember it in my imagination. It's an interesting distinction, but it's a valid way of receiving psychic information, and it works for me. Similarly, some people can 'see' angels and deceased loved ones as clear as day, right in front of them. But truthfully, those people are few and far between. Many other people get their clairvoyant communications through images in their imagination, either with eyes closed or open. It's similar to recalling a scene from your favorite movie. The images aren't 'visual' in the perfect/pure/I-see-you-with-my-eyes sense, but again, the messages received that way are valid and can be trusted.

It is my hope that this chapter gives you the courage, conviction and compassion to work with your friends, loved ones and even strangers when they are near transi-tion. You have so many tools at your disposal: prayer, energy work, intuition, love. The blessings of doing this work are vast, emotionally rewarding and priceless.

◇

Secret Language

Your angels ask you to notice the
symbols and signs all around you.

Having asked for guidance and
reassurance, pay attention to the secret
language of the world around you.
Signs that your loved ones are nearby
may come in the form of a butterfly,
a feather or a coin appearing
on your path.

CHRISTINE SCHREIBSTEIN
Baltimore, Maryland, USA

CHRISTINE SCHREIBSTEIN has been chatting with the angels for as long as she can remember and using the angelic humor, love and wisdom to enhance not only her life, but those around her.

Among her many certifications, Christine resonates mostly as Archangel Enlightenment Therapist and Soul Coach. She has melded all of her trainings, readings, and life experiences together to create a formula that allows clients to step out of their own way so they may embrace and manifest the life they not only desire, but deserve.

Christine contributed a chapter to the book *Soul Whispers II*, has articles published on More.com and her upcoming book, *The GABI Life: Bringing joy, love and grace back to your daily life through the wisdom of a dog*, will certainly delight many.

Christine wishes you a wondrous day filled with great joy and angel hugs!

You may find more information about Christine and her services at www. AngelChatter.com

Chatting with the Angels

CHRISTINE SCHREIBSTEIN

Look for and embrace joy, laughter and giggles throughout each day.
Be exuberant in knowing that the angels are here to assist you,
for angels can be everywhere at a moment's notice.

*A*ngels have always and will always be with us. So who are these entities, energies, creatures? The loose definition of angel means *Messenger of God.* Therefore, the very essence of their identity means communication. How can the doors of communication open more fully so we may communicate regularly with them? Does your state of mind hinder or help? (hint: it does) Can you use tools to open the doors of communication? (You sure can!) Lastly, how will they choose to communicate with you? (Get ready for the magic!)

You desire to communicate, converse and chat with the angels, and yet this seems to evade you. Why? The reasons can be simple, but quite ingrained. The first could be a deep-seated belief that you are not worthy to receive messages from the angelic realm. Before you argue this point, think about it. If you knew that there was an angel standing next to you at this very moment in full regalia of wings, halo and flowing gown, would you feel tingles of apprehension and slightly overwhelmed? Perhaps you might even be frightened, wondering why you have been singled out for this great event. Would you wonder – why me? OR would you rush to their open and loving arms to embrace them with great love and joy?

Are you worthy of such a visitation?

The answer is quite simply, a resounding YES! You are most deserving. You are loving. You are joyful. You are truly fantastic! Truth be told, there probably *is* an angel standing next to you at this very moment. Now that you know this, can you accept their presence? Gently close your eyes and relax into the energies that are being given to you. Feel the love that is emanating, and feel the safety and security of their presence. Simply breathe in this beautiful, loving moment. Relish it. Own it. You are worthy to receive this now and whenever you desire. Just remember this:

You Are Worthy

Chatting with the angels can be a rather easy process. Unfortunately, as humans, we tend to make it more difficult and detailed oriented than it really needs to be. Many people are in the mindset that if something is worth having, hard work must be undertaken in order to obtain it. Not true! Following are some ways to remember how to relax, accept and ultimately chat with the angels as often as you desire, as well as to remind you how accessible the angels are and how effortless the process is.

The first example is a child. Children are wonderful teachers in the art of staying in the present moment while expecting great things to happen. For them, everything and anything is possible. Do you remember how you could play for hours using your imagination as the primary source? You could be a magician, a princess, and even go on a ride within a spaceship. You were full of possibilities and nobody could tell you differently. You were one with the world and loved every moment of it. You were truly connected to the angelic realm because you allowed the process to *unfold in pure joy and consciousness*.

Think of a time in your past that brought you great joy. This moment allowed you to feel whole, loved, joyful and incredible! As you begin to remember this moment, recall as many details as possible. What aromas were present? Were there flowers? Was there something baking or cooking? Can you hear the noises, the laughter, the chatting that fills in this memory? How about clothing? What were you wearing? What were others wearing? What were the colors of the area surrounding you? Let the memories swell within your body, bringing with it the joy, the peace and the empowerment of that time.

As you are reliving those memories, place your hands gently over your solar plexus. Notice how your body is reacting to these wonderful memories. It feels more expansive as the emotions wash over you. Your mind becomes still. Your heart expands as it brings in the happiness and joy. You love feeling this way. Your body confirms this by elongating with grace. You sigh as the emotions settle. You smile. Savor your feelings, your powers and your emotions. As you remove your hands, the state of happiness remains. Know that with a little practice you can obtain this state whenever you desire. To get to this place again, it may help to repeat this exercise, reliving this memory, placing your hands on your solar plexus and reveling in the emotions. This repetitive practice is reminding you of what this feels like. Your body loves feeling centered, expanded, and whole. With practice, you will be able to feel like this whenever and wherever you wish. However, take your time; *enjoy the process* of opening those doors to make chatting with your angels both easy and joyful.

Another possible tool is to re-establish your relationship with your imaginary friend. Whether you remember having one or not, odds are you did, especially if you feel a kinship with the angels now as an adult. I myself had forgotten about mine until several years ago while having a session with an intuitive. Archangel Ariel was called in as part of our session together. Before I could stop myself, I yelled out "PINKY!" I quickly covered my mouth in embarrassment and shock, and even looked around me hoping it was somebody else who had yelled. Unfortunately it was me. However, even more fortunately it WAS me, for I had just reconnected with my imaginary friend that I'd long ago forgotten. You see, Archangel Ariel is pink in her color resonance and therefore I had given her the very appropriate name of Pinky. She reappeared in my cognitive mind when I least expected it. I wasn't forcing a situation to happen; it was allowed to unfold of its own accord. Hmmm . . . there is a theme beginning to unfold; *allow the process to happen* instead of trying to force a result.

If you are unsure if you had an imaginary friend, place your hands over your heart. Inhale and exhale slowly three times. Ask yourself, "Did I have an imaginary friend?" If you cannot remember or don't get a clear response, don't berate yourself. Opening the door to remember those times will lead you to reconnecting with them once again. Remember this little trick: "I know you don't remember your imaginary friend, but if you did, what would you remember?"

If you do remember, make it more vivid and alive by asking questions such as: What do you see? What do they look like? What is their name? What kind of conversations or games did you participate in together? The list is endless, *allow the process to unfold* and you will get more answers than you realized you had questions for!

There are many other ways to tangibly connect with the angels once again. One of these is through the use of crystals. Crystals assist us in many arenas such as health, abundance, joy and even angelic chatting. While there are specific crystals that connect with specific angels, there are also crystals with a primary purpose to open the portals of the angelic realm.

Do you need a crystal in order to chat with the angels? Absolutely not, but the crystals do offer a tangible reminder of your ability to chat with the angelic realm. Working with

Playfulness

Your ability to laugh and relax allows you to be more open to your angels' guidance.

Take time for regular periods of playfulness. By letting go of your cares and allowing yourself more playtime you will feel more relaxed. This attracts positive experiences into your life and helps you to connect with your angels.

crystals tends to open doors for their users. One of the reasons, or philosophies, is that the pressure is no longer on the user alone to make the connection. They can relax and 'let the crystal do its work,' thus allowing chatting in its various forms to commence and unfold. Make no mistake, crystals do assist. They all have unique properties, just as your talents are different from mine. The common theme of the crystal kingdom is that, amongst many other possibilities, they offer enlightenment, joy and harmony.

The first splendid crystal to be addressed is Selenite. Selenite is a beautiful opaque crystal that is available in many colors, but most prominently found in tones of white. It has striations, or layers, of fine crystals that have melded together over the years to create a luminescent crystal that seems to glow from within. Selenite can be found in a polished form as well as its natural state. Both the natural and polished are equal in their clarity of assisting your connection with the angels. It is truly a personal preference. Note: If you obtain one, please never put Selenite in water for it will dissolve!

Working, playing or simply having Selenite around you begins to gently open your senses to the angelic realm while making the connection strong and loving, as it is meant to be. Selenite can also help alleviate any blockages that are preventing you from reconnecting with the angels while assisting you in moving forward and not becoming stagnant in any situation. Life would be very boring indeed if we stayed put and never wanted to move forward in any area of our life! We personally have Selenite in various places throughout our home – under chairs that we use in the living quarters as well as underneath our bed. Do they work? I cannot definitely say, except that I love chatting with the angels whenever I wish!

Another enchanting crystal is Celestite. Celestite is a soft crystal that tends to be a light blue in color; however, it may also be found in shades of gold. Celestite works lovingly with you as you reach for the stars, specifically the angels, while living your life in a very serene, yet focused manner. It assists to dissolve any obstruction that is not allowing natural chatting between you and the angelic realm, specifically with your guardian angel. It radiates soft waves of energy while gently cleansing the area surrounding it. We have a piece of Celestite in our kitchen area. It truly helps to keep the energies of the heated kitchen calm, loving and open to endless possibilities of creative cooking while chatting with the angels. What a yummy combination!

The last exquisite crystal to be suggested is Angel Aura Quartz. While there are some that don't think this is a real crystal, there are many, including me, that love its energies and how it assists. Why the discrepancy? Angel Aura Quartz is actually a clear quartz crystal that has been infused at extremely high temperatures with the mineral of platinum. The purists within the crystal kingdom do not consider this man-made blending authentic, and tend to disregard the healing and energy properties that Angel Aura Quartz can offer. If you are not one of them, you will be glad to know that the blending of platinum and clear quartz creates a beautiful opalish glazing on the crystal that creates a loving, compassionate and high energy crystal.

Angel Aura Quartz brings with it a calming of the mind, serenity and peace. It helps to open and reconnect you with the angelic realm while releasing issues from past lives and attuning you more with your spiritual purpose in this current lifetime. Angel Aura Quartz assists its user in seeing beauty in all that they encounter. This opens the door of gratitude wider which then also opens the door for easier access to the angels. We have this one in our home office area and find it very beneficial as we write creatively.

In what ways will your angel(s) decide to connect with you? The ways are as varied as there as angels, but typically this will come delivered in the best and most natural way for you to accept. You may *smell* an aroma that has no sense of belonging in that moment – a strong floral scent in the basement for example. You may have a *sense of knowing* what to do or not to do next. You may literally *hear* them chatting in your ears offering guidance. Within your mind you may *see* the next step. You may *taste* (rather unusual, but possible) your answer. You may *feel* what to do. Out of those mentioned, there is one that will be the most natural for you. However, you may not always receive your message in that format. Keep in mind that the forms of communication do span the spectrum and may alter depending on the circumstances, your mood, and the day.

A situation may require more unusual methods to make you pay attention. For example, my mother remembers a day when she was younger. She was driving down the road and had passed a car. She was slightly day-dreaming and remained in the passing lane. She clearly heard, *"Move over, NOW."* Without thinking she promptly did, and shortly thereafter a car appeared around the bend that would have hit her head on. Her audible command was rather unusual in that she and her infant son were the only ones in the car. It got her attention and fast. We are grateful that she listened so quickly!

There is a time and a place for all, but trust is the key to keeping the lines of communication open. *Trust in the process.* Trust in the releasing of the mindset that you have to do everything by yourself. Trust that you will always be taken care of. Listen to what your body tells you it needs. *Allow the process to happen.* Follow your guidance. Listen and relax into the energies of the angels, the loving, wise and humorous angels. They do love to laugh and they do love to make you laugh, because laughing immediately connects you with them.

Reflect on that: laughing connects you with the angels.

When you laugh, you feel expansive, joyous, not a care in the world. Why wouldn't the angels use this as a tool to help you to chat with them? Be joyous in your chatting attempts. Be happy in the mere knowledge that angels do exist. Look for and embrace joy, laughter and giggles throughout each day. Be exuberant in knowing that the angels are here to assist you, for angels can be everywhere at a moment's notice.

I wish to share a personal story that drove home this concept, for me at least. After my "Pinky" experience, I began to read more and more about the angels. I became curious. Who else could be one of my current angel guides? When I was serious (therefore not allowing the process to unfold naturally), I would constantly ask. No answer came. I demanded an answer. None came. I got frustrated and stomped my feet. That of course didn't help. I stopped asking. (I'll show them who's boss!) While traveling on a ferry to meet family, I was in one of those moods beyond giddiness. I was elated, flying high and felt connected to the boat I was on, to the jellyfish in the water and to all of the passengers. I was perhaps a bit flippant in my high energies, but I was laughing and enjoying life to the fullest. So I thought I would try once more and asked, "So if you are really with me, what's your name?"

Without hesitation, the name "Ezekiel" came to me. Now I don't know about you, but Ezekiel is not part of my regular name group and would not have been the name I would have conjured up in my mind. Hmmm . . . That surprised me and yet because of the unusual name I knew it was real. Wow, I had more than one angel with me? I've come to realize that we all do, but this was indeed a revelation at the time. I was in a moment of joy and because of that joy, the answers came quickly and I was able to hear. Does that mean you always have to be joyful, silly or beyond giddy? No, of course not, but initially it does help to go to the other extreme. In due time, your internal pendulum will bring you back to a natural center – the center where you experience expansive joy and can acknowledge the not-so-joyful moments with more personal detachment. Breathe, relax and have fun with the angels. That is their strongest desire for you:

Enjoy your life and all that you do.

Will I ever see an angel? You may, then again, you may already have and not realized it. All is possible. You may see them as they are depicted: flowing robes, arms outreached, glowing. You may encounter them as an animal that comes to your side to calm you when you feel threatened, insecure or simply in need of some unconditional love. It may be a stranger that assists you in a moment of need. How the angels choose to let themselves be known to you is as varied as the number of people reading this. Everyone has a different connotation of what an angel 'should' be. Everyone has a different level of what they expect and will accept. Everyone is living a different experience that brings with it a wide group of people or animals that they would naturally encounter.

For example, if a stranger offered to buy you coffee at your local cafe and then started to chat with you, it might seem rather odd and you may rebuff the offer. However, if you are in a foreign country and a local begins a conversation with you about the area, in your language, you may be more inclined to accept this little bit of help. This very encounter happened to us years ago as we were traveling in Italy. My husband was doing research for a book about the Italian participation in World War II and had located the oldest Synagogue in Rome. As he was telling me about the Synagogue, an elderly man came over to us and for more than 20 minutes told us information about the building and its participation in the war that would have been difficult, if not impossible to find at a later date or via regular means of investigation. This man was delightful in his demeanor. Short in stature, he had an impish air about him with a twinkle in his eye. He was pure joy to chat with. Our conversation slowly came to an end and he waved us on in good humor. As we were walking away, my husband looked at me and said, "I bet you think he was an angel, don't you?"

"Perhaps, but it is more important that you do," was my retort. When I turned around, our heavenly friend waved, winked and disappeared.

In closing, remember that *you are worthy* to receive any and all forms of communication with the angelic realm today and always. *Allow the process* to unfold for you. How the angels choose to connect will vary. Simply be open and enjoy the glorious ride you are embarking upon. Have fun chatting with the angels. Enjoy, relish and bask in the love, the wisdom, the joy and the heavenly embraces that are being offered to you daily. Allow them to assist you in your life's journey and you will never be lead astray.

Journey to meet your Guardian Angel

The following is a guided meditation that opens the doors of communication between you and your guardian angel or any angel you wish to connect with. If you choose to record the words for easier meditative purposes, feel free to add or substitute your own words or add an angel's name. This meditation is meant for you, so please make it yours. By making the meditation easy to speak and then listen to, you will be more inclined to relax and enjoy the process. For example, the setting is in the woods, but perhaps you are more of an ocean person. Feel free to change the scenery. It will in no way harm or affect your results. In fact, by going with the surroundings that you feel a closer kinship with, you will be able to ease and flow along the path of meeting and connecting with the angels.

Add candles if you wish. Play music. Instrumental music is recommended for obvious reasons. You may desire to hold one of the crystals mentioned earlier in this chapter. Do what is necessary for you in order to make the most of this meditation. By doing so, you will relax into the process with greater ease which of course will only lead to more joy, and isn't that the desired result after all? Joyful connection!

Sit or lie down in a very comfortable position.

Inhale gently and deeply through your nose. Feel the air expanding your lower rib cage and filtering down to your toes.

Exhale softly through your mouth, releasing any doubts, concerns and random thoughts.

Inhale again, feeling your shoulders relax and your mind slowing.

Now exhale, further relaxing your body and mind.

One last time, inhale deeply through your nose, bringing the center of your focus to your heart and third eye, joining the two together in beautiful harmony.

Exhale and release an audible "ahhhh . . ." feeling your body deepen into a safe and secure meditative state.

Continue breathing as you slowly count backwards from ten to one. When you reach five, the room noises are more subtle. You only hear the noises that are necessary for you to meet your angel. When you reach one, you are now completely relaxed and ready to venture forth. You see before you a beautiful clearing nestled in the woods. The trees are fully leafed out creating areas of shade, allowing warm patches of gentle sunlight where needed. The butterflies are flitting with the gentle breeze as it caresses your skin and hair. You hear birds singing as they invite the day into their lives. You feel energized.

You feel safe.

You feel joy.

You feel love.

As you walk through the clearing, you see before you a large log. This log is long and rests comfortably and securely on the ground. Green grass hugs the log, growing up around it, making the log appear more inviting. Flowers are nestled in crevices and beckon to you. You know that this log will support and protect you while offering comfort and beauty. As you approach, you realize your angel is sitting upon the log waiting for you. Your angel is beautiful, more beautiful than you have ever imagined. This angel is everything you ever desired in color, scent and spirit. They invite you to sit beside them.

You approach the log and your angel willingly. As you sit, your angel asks if you have any questions. Of course you do! You have been preparing for this meeting for a long time. As the questions pour out of you, your angel takes your hand in theirs and loving answers each and every question in quiet contemplation and without rushing. Time is an illusion and you have all the time that is required for this and all future meetings together.

You laugh together. You rest your head on their shoulder and they hold you tight. You allow their strength, their love and their joy to wash over you. They are thrilled to have you so close again and remind you that they are never far away. In fact, they are only a mere thought, a hint of a thought away, and it just takes a simple yearning from you and they are with you. This knowledge is now fully integrated within you and will never be forgotten again.

It is time for this meeting to end and for you to return back to the present day. Your embrace slowly ends. They kiss you lightly on your forehead and whisper softly in your ear, "You are loved." As you look into their eyes, you remember everything.

You rise from the log and begin to walk away. You turn; your angel sits there patiently, lovingly watching you walk back through the meadow. You resume your walk back to the present moment.

You now begin to count from one to ten. Slowly you return to the present. As you reach five, you feel the chair and floor supporting you, your fingers and toes begin to move and you hear the noises within and around the room you are in. When you reach ten, you are fully present in the here and now. You feel completely relaxed, cognizant and grounded.

You inhale deeply, then loudly exhale, bringing with that exhale all the information you gained from your meeting and anchoring you more fully within your body.

Your eyes open.

You smile with the knowledge that:

You are loved, always and in all ways.

∽

ROS BOOTH
Perth, Western Australia

ROS IS AN accomplished Angel Intuitive™, Weight Loss and Health Coach and Psychic Healer who lives in sunny Perth, Western Australia. Ros has welfare and degree studies in Human Services and Community Development. With a compassionate nature and good humor Ros has spent many years in service organizations providing assistance to many disadvantaged community members including those facing domestic violence, long term unemployment and poverty. With a passion for sharing knowledge and improving the wellbeing of children, Ros also spent many years developing and working in children's organizations and committees.

Like many other lightworkers, Ros comes from a psychic matriarchy but kept her gifts quiet due to societal values. With a private, personal history peppered with challenges, pain and emotional upheaval Ros has not always felt safe about sharing her unseen gifts. However, like fine wine, Ros's psychic abilities only grew stronger with age and eventually Ros trusted and pursued her new divine life pathway.

Today, Ros uses her vast welfare knowledge and personal return to health experiences to underpin her current practice in providing health and weight loss coaching and workshops. Ros now specializes in food insensitivities and HcG coaching drawing on her many eclectic skills to provide individualized readings and support. She enjoys inspiring and igniting the lights she sees shining within each and every one of us, and travels the world facilitating workshops and conducting personal client sessions. To book an individual session or check her workshop schedule, contact Ros at AngelMagicRos@yahoo.com

Let Your Light Shine

ROS BOOTH

And as we let our light shine,
we unconsciously give other people permission to do the same.
As we are liberated from our own fear,
our presence automatically liberates others.

—MARIANNE WILLIAMSON

The Decision

I stepped as fast as I could on the treadmill, the chords to my heart swaying from the exertion. "You're doing well, Ros!" the doctor exclaimed. But I knew otherwise; I could barely breathe. The doctor helped me off the treadmill and checked the monitors as I regained my composure.

It was March. I had just turned 47 and my health had recently taken another downward turn. Now, I was undergoing yet another heart test as doctors tried to figure out what was wrong with me. In truth, I already knew what the problem was: over forty years of living with a shield of fat over my body had caught up with me. I was obese. I knew deep in my heart that I had to make a definitive choice: either get my life and body in check, or leave the planet. And I knew I had to decide immediately.

Intuitively I knew that the doctors would not find anything majorly wrong. The angels around me were sending me this last warning so I would finally pay attention. As I drove home, panic rose in my chest. I had to find a way to lose weight and get fit as quickly as possible. I asked – no, I pleaded – with the angels for help. With tears in my eyes, I sent up my prayer: "Please help me!"

The next few months were marked with the assistance of angels of every sort – from traditional Heavenly angels and fairies to incarnated earth angels who helped me survive, and finally, thrive. This is my journey back to life.

Finding Help

I explored many options but found that most retreats were just fancy spas. The lack of facilities to help someone lose weight was discouraging. Then an email arrived with a referral to a program in a different state – a boot camp designed specifically for people like me, over 100 kg. It was just what I was looking for! But, I could feel the fearful resistance rising once again in my gut. What if it didn't work?

Racing to errands, my fears cramped my thoughts. *Will this be the right place?*

Will it be worth the money? Will I get the results I need? The questions spun in my mind like a centrifuge. All my life, I had used my excess weight to dim my capacity. I was afraid of how much more intuitive I really was. It wasn't just the weight I needed to drop. I needed to drop my fears of being who *I am*. It was time to be a happy *and* intuitive person. I gripped the steering wheel harder as I contemplated my decision. "Angels, I need some signs that this is the right decision!" I declared firmly. It was rare for me to make such a direct request for myself from my angelic crowd, but today I needed to know for sure.

I kept driving, in a state of mild anxiety until I pulled up at the next red light. An unusual number plate suddenly caught my attention: *UUU: Victoria The Place To Be*. I blinked in disbelief. Victoria was where the Boot Camp was! I felt a chuckle rise up from my belly; I laughed, heartily releasing the stress I had felt. I thanked the angels for their quick response, feeling safe with their angelic guidance, and commenced my preparations for a life changing journey.

The Journey

Flying into Melbourne I released my seatbelt as the captain announced the chilly temperature outside was four degrees Celsius. I felt a flutter of excitement ripple across my solar plexus. Picking up my luggage I braced myself for the cold, and the start of my "New and Wonderful Me" journey. Meeting me with a sisterly hug, Prue embraced me with welcoming encouragement before she drove the final leg of the journey to drop me at the retreat. She was a fellow Angel Intuitive™ and gifted earth angel, and I felt blessed to have her support.

The Boot Camp organizers had made an unexpected change of venue; the uncertainty of change made me nervous. However, Prue's soft energy calmly exuded an enveloping cloud of safety, dissipating my anxiety. As we drove through the beautiful brick gates, my eye caught sight of the address number *1444*. It was another sign from the angels! I had read in Doreen Virtue's *Angel Numbers* book that angels use numbers as a way to communicate signs, and that 444 indicates "You are surrounded by angels." Peace replaced tension.

Sturdy pine trees lined the fence like a mini forest and we saw dozens of huge fairy toadstools, the kind I remembered from Enid Blyton books. I could feel the fairies' welcome and both Prue and I exclaimed unison surprise and joy. I knew I was in the right place and that the fairy elementals were here to help everyone to manifest health, recovery, and new lives.

Weight loss expert Alex greeted us with his sparkling brown eyes and a sincere, welcoming smile. He had been a previous weight loss contestant for a famous reality show. His own personal journey and angelic guidance led him to his life's purpose: helping people recover from severe obesity.

He called us up individually for a starting photo and weigh-in. Most of us were shockingly embarrassed and sad as the weights were called out. When it was my turn, the number 147.7 kg flashed on a screen next to me, while Alex read the total aloud. My eyes welled with tears and I choked away a feeling of grief. I had been much heavier in the past, but the reality of what I looked like and weighed hit hard. Then Alex told me that according to my body statistics, my biological age was 84 – not my actual age of 47. I felt startled, but I wasn't surprised – I'd felt very close to the end of my time when I was guided to come here. In fact, I was quite familiar with that 84-year-old shadow within me. I knew her well. It wasn't just the physical effects of the obesity that haunted me. I feared the shadow's incessant pull toward the grave, beguiling me to give in, surrender. Today, I drew a firm line in the sand.

The morning's embarrassment became a distant memory later in bed that night, lying sore and exhausted. I relished the early lights-out, but just as my eyes seemed to barely shut, the alarm rudely interrupted my peaceful sleep at 5:30 a.m. My new running shoes challenged me as I contorted to painfully reach my feet. Blinking away the redness in my face, I headed out to the gym to meet with several personal trainers and commence the grueling training.

"One, two – miss a few – one hundred!" I yelled loudly, trying to muster some humor as I plodded along at one of the lowest speeds on the treadmill. Onward I marched, letting myself off every few minutes to sit on a fit ball and relax the cramping in my lower back. My humor faded as the pain escalated until it felt like a hot poker scorching through my body. All other muscle pain seemed to fade in the background in contrast, and all I felt was agony. While everyone else experienced delayed onset muscle soreness, the dreaded DOMS, I could only focus on my body that felt 84 years old and its never-ending pain. That night I went to bed early, creaking into bed, tucking pillows under my legs.

"Gottagetup! Gottagetup! Gottagetup!" the alarm seemed to screech at me again the next morning. I lifted my eyelids to a dark room and felt momentarily confused. *It's night time! No, its time to get up!* The pain enveloping my joints rolled out of bed with me. But I was not going to be beaten! I was here to change. I dressed as quickly as I could, ignoring the protests and pain of that persistent 84-year-old shadow. She was not in charge. *I was.*

Outside a blanket of stars sparkled overhead; the sun blinking through the misty clouds along the horizon. Fog settled comfortably across the paddocks. I tried hard to enjoy the beauty before me which I usually missed from sleeping in. Despite my snail's pace I was soon panting and chuffing like an old lady. Then that familiar hot poker of pain seared through my hips and back – clearly my body was not coping well. Hot tears streamed from my eyes and rolled down my red, puffy face. How would I accomplish the day's work ahead of me? I pleaded silently *Angels, please help me!* as I continued to step slowly, painfully. Soon, I could feel them all around me – a comforting cloud of love and energy. I breathed in this angelic support and thought about all my family, guides, angels, and earth angel friends supporting me. The soft, early-morning breeze swept gently across my cheeks, like the feathery touch of angels stroking away my tears. I breathed in the love and support. I walked some more. And with the help of my angels, I made it through the first part of the morning.

Our next session was an outdoor circuit medley. *This can't be too hard!* I naively thought to myself. Then our personal trainer, aptly nicknamed "The Gavinator," announced we had to do thirty sets of each activity. *Thirty?! Surely he'll modify that number for me!* I thought with alarm as I looked around at the group. We varied greatly in age and fitness level. I was by far the largest participant. My hips quivered at the thought of doing thirty sets, but I was focused on a wave of panic that had snuck into my body.

By the time we arrived at the course, my hips and back had tightened with shock and resistance to what lay ahead. My head was muddled, and uncertainty prevailed. How on earth was I going to manage? But onwards I went, each step sending jolts of pain rising in intensity with every effort. After climbing up and down a fence twenty times, I faced The Gavinator. "I can't do anymore!" I declared pitifully. "No, another ten," he firmly stated. Reluctantly, I stepped up and down the fence, holding back tears of pain and hopelessness.

Healing

Your angels ask that you release all challenges to them for healing.

Knowing that all is in Divine order, hold loving thoughts for yourself as you visualize the situation as already healed. Release all fears and perceived challenges to your angels. For in truth, you are both healer and healed.

Moving to the next activity we were beside the fairy glen, and I knew it was time to call in reinforcements. "Please help me!" I pleaded silently to the fairies. "Please help me!"

I struggled, focusing on putting one foot ahead of the other and breathing through the searing pain. Finally, a miracle – The Gavinator moved me along to the next task. Filled with gratitude, I thanked the fairies for helping me to be seen as I hobbled to the next station. Each step caused waves of pain throughout my body as I approached the next activity. When the time came to begin, I found myself rooted in place with tears overwhelming my will. The Gavinator quietly excused me from repeating the activities.

Ashamed and relieved, I shuffled my way back to the gym to wait for everyone. I was deeply disappointed that the terrible pain held me back. That 84-year-old shadow, the part of me that was so close to death, seemed determined to hang on to her old body. She seemed to have hold of me with ancient, creaking fingers of steel. But I had steel within me, as well – I had a *will* of steel. I was *determined* to live!

And so this is how many of my days went, at night resting deeply and repeating positive affirmations in my mind. I met messages of support and hope with gasps of joy. I relished each text and replayed each voice message encouraging me to continue. My days passed in a haze of agony and sweat. My sleep was haunted. I had to run to the bathroom every few hours, and painful hips broke my sleep almost continuously. By the end of my first week, my spirit was frazzled. I almost felt like I could not go on.

But another earth angel crossed my path in the guise of the retreat's chiropractor – a gentleman of retirement age with a corny wit, a sparkle in his eyes and a quick, generous smile. I was somewhat skeptical, imagining he would bend me and crack me into weird and unimaginable positions. When he showed me his little tool for tapping on pressure points, I felt more confident. In a matter of minutes I left the table and felt the pain practically melt away. That night, I slept most of the night, and the next day, felt like the hand of God had touched me with a miracle. My hips were truly pain free! I had turned a corner.

The next morning I found myself stepping slowly but confidently up a slightly hilly street. I listened to the *Hurrah!* from kookaburras in overhanging trees. A small creek trickled nearby, and the speckled light of the sunrise was greeted by the sounds of ducks landing for a morning wash. I relished these moments as beautiful distractions from the exertions of my body.

I began the second week feeling stiff, but confident. The classes seemed easier. However, my attitude changed a few hours later when we ventured to an athletic park to attempt laps. *I can't do this! I'll have to sit this one out,* I thought to myself. My accompanying fit ball bounced with reassurance.

But in *this* program, "I can't" is not an option. I was sent with the group to the starting line. "This is an endurance race of 1,600 meters. Four laps around the track", the trainer advised. *There is no way I'm getting around even one lap, let alone four!* I thought glumly as I headed off. Approaching the first lap I grew slightly more optimistic. Shuffling along, I gauged the distance and thought; *maybe I can make it two laps . . .* Normally needing to sit every few minutes I was nervous, so four times around the track without stopping seemed unrealistic. As I passed the finish line the first time, the trainers offered lots of encouragement.

"You can do this, Ros! Keep going!" Their encouragement bolstered me. As I panted and started to struggle, I found myself searching deep within. I started to chant my personal mantra of affirmations to myself – *I can feel my body getting stronger! I can do this!*

I can feel my body getting stronger! I can do this! Over and over I repeated this to myself and eventually I was heading to the start line for the third time. Other participants had finished and started to add words of encouragement as I approached. "Well done, Ros!" "You can do it, Ros!" Starting my last lap, I noticed I was joined by another guest. "C'mon, Ros! Let's do this last lap together! I'm with you now," she said warmly. I was humbled by her encouragement, moving as fast as I could. I huffed my way across the finish line and collapsed onto the bulging fit ball to rest my back as my fellow exercisers surrounded me, congratulating me. I had completed all four laps in twenty-five minutes. I felt like I had really done something amazing.

"Now it's time to do sprints!" the trainer announced. I choked on my water. Surely, he had lost his mind? Maybe I'd heard him wrong. "Fifty meters! Line up!" he shouted.

Oh my god, he isn't joking. My classmates were already waiting at the start line. I, on the other hand, was still sprawled across my fit ball out of breath. "I can't sprint!" I wailed at the trainer in protest. My old resistant habit spoke for me. "*I can't* do that!" "Then just walk, Ros." he replied unsympathetically. Disappointment rushed into my body. The thought of being last was again embarrassing me. I felt invisible, that my needs were ignored. *Can't they give me a rest first? I haven't even caught my breath from the laps!*

My achievement vanished as I stood in my lane, wondering how I was going to manage a sprint!

"Go!" Everyone took off with a whoosh. *It's like we're racing to a Myer Christmas sale!* I mused dreamily. Then I realized that *my* legs were shuffling along at top speed, far faster than I ever thought capable. I noticed my embarrassment fade, and I left the surprised old woman gasping at the starting line as the real Ros flew down the track. I moved faster and faster, the pavement slipping beneath me. My wobbly legs seemed to possess a will of their own. Down the track, I became aware of the three excited trainers. Most of my classmates were already at the finish line, staring at me. They stared with an unfamiliar mix of stunned shock and surprise. "Ros is running!" I heard someone yell. "Ros!" "Hey, you're running!" I must have crossed the finish line, because everyone was surrounding me, applauding, and someone announced my time as 17 seconds. Seventeen seconds! Miracles truly *are* real.

The miraculous breakthrough caused a stirring. Sure, I had run. But now the 84-year-old shadow was back, as bitter and nasty as ever. As the next few days' activities became even more challenging, I could feel the pain in my hips and back flare up once again. It felt like that shadow was digging her steely fingers into my bones with relentless strength, determined to wear me down. "I told you so! I told you that you couldn't do it!" my body seemed to say. The pain made my days almost unbearable and I woke day after day feeling defeated. But I kept on showing up to classes, going through the motions.

Two weeks had passed and I was back in the main hall where I had started my journey, surrounded by my classmates – now my friends. With a deep breath I faced the scale. I had melted 5 kg of actual fat! Even better news – I had reduced my biological age to 79!

I breathed a sigh of relief and joined the activities of the last two weeks with a new sense of vigor and determination. I was not fazed when the 79-year-old shadow tripped me up and I twisted my ankle. I was running. Her sabotaging did not stop or deter me.

The Light Shines

I awoke on my last week filled with joy. Art therapy was scheduled for today. My creative side had been yearning for an outlet, so I played with the paints with glee. As I painted the highs and lows of my journey, I became aware yet again of a pattern that I initially noticed during my journaling over the previous month. *Even in the darkest and most fractured times, my light still glows,* I remembered my notes as I painted. *In the darkest tunnel, the seemingly endless blackness is always lit with the light within me.* I grabbed a fresh sheet of paper and started painting with bright yellow. *I have my own light to illuminate my path.* And then, my real breakthrough: *I am the only one who dims my light! I only dim it from myself!* This new sense of awareness glowed within me and I could feel my energy expand and my aura sparkle. I liked the emergence of my new and real me, and joyfully painted my glowing, illuminated self.

The next morning, I awoke feeling like an excited child – I was going to meet my dear cousin, Louise, at a festival. I hadn't seen her in 25 years. Louise is a well-known psychic and medium, and I was extremely grateful for the timing of our meeting. Turning a corner, I spotted her beaming smile. I raced to give her a hug, and we melted into each other's arms with joyful love. When it was time to finally leave, Louise lifted an item from her table, saying, "I have something for you." She placed in my hands a laminated paper with a beautiful poem, which I immediately recognized as a quote from Marianne Williamson: *Our deepest fear is not that we are inadequate. Our deepest fear is that we are powerful beyond measure. It is our light, not our darkness that most frightens us . . .*

I was overjoyed to receive such a beautiful gift. I had been trying all my life to dampen my light, and here my earth angel cousin was recognizing that it was time for me to move forward. I felt truly blessed and honored. I read the poem over and over, the last line catching my fullest attention:

> *As we are liberated from our own fear,*
> *our presence automatically liberates others.*

It was in that moment that I felt the old 79-year-old shadow's fingers release from my body forever. I had allowed that old shadow to grow large and to overpower my true light. But she could not hold substance as the true light within me brightly glowed. I proved that to her, and my true self, when I returned to the track a few days later for the endurance test. I shaved a whole three minutes off my original time and one second off the sprint.

Today, I am still on my weight loss and recovery journey. I allow my Light to Shine brightly, with the courage to now live my true purpose!

Letting Your Light Shine Exercises

We have all had experiences that have led us to stray from our true selves – sometimes momentarily, sometimes for a lifetime. Some experiences are so frightening, we entirely forget who we really are. The forgetting is supposed to keep us safe. But in truth, we are always safe, one with the divine.

These exercises are designed to help you reflect on your true magnificence, your bright light. You came here to Earth to be happy and joyful. Whether you wish to lose weight, be happier, find a new career or just a new direction, discovering who you are and letting your inner light guide you is one of the first steps to realizing your goals.

Safe Space

The first step is to create a safe space – a quiet place where you can be on your own for between 30 and 60 minutes. Turn off the phones if you can and let your loved ones know this is your sacred time. In this quiet area, surround yourself with relaxing and encouraging pictures, crystals, statues, and other sacred items. Play some high-vibration music to help set the mood for being at rest and to connect with your inner light. You will also need a journal and writing materials.

Getting in Touch with the Real You – Your Inner Light

Take the time to close your eyes and take in a very deep breath, in through the nose and down into your lower belly. Breathe out all your concerns and worries through your mouth with an "Aaaaggh." Repeat this again and feel yourself grow relaxed and peaceful. Imagine you are surrounded by the loving energy of all your guardian angels, spirit guides and Archangel Michael, protecting and guiding you. Scan your body and notice your entire senses. Relax further and just be present. Keep breathing deeply into your belly. You can hear the sounds around you: the relaxing music and your breath as it passes in and out of your body.

When the moment feels right, take your journal in hand and start to write a reflection to yourself, with no judgments or criticism. The following questions can be a starting point:

If there were no limitations, what do I imagine I would be doing?

What makes my heart sing?

What does my inner light look like? (You may wish to use separate paper and draw a picture)

What does my Inner Light need me to do to shine at my best?

How and to whom will my Lightliness be of benefit?

Make Lists

My final exercise is one I share from the teachings of Abraham, as channeled through Esther Hicks.

"Make lists of positive aspects. Make lists of things you love – and never complain about anything. And as you use those things that shine bright and make you feel good as your excuse to give your attention to and be *who-you-are,* you will tune to *who-you-are,* and the whole world will begin to transform before your eyes. *It is not your job to transform the world for others – but it is your job to transform it for you. A state of appreciation is pure Connection to Source where there is no perception of lack."*

It is always safe to be you. I wish you much love and blessings of joy on your own journey, as you *Let Your Light Shine.*

∾

Bibliography

Hicks, E and J. *Money and the Law of Attraction: Learning to Attract Health, Wealth and Happiness.* Hay House Inc, 2008.

Williamson, M. *A Course in Weight*: *21 Spiritual Lessons for Surrendering Your Weight Forever,* Hay House, 2010.

Williamson, M. *A Return to Love: Reflections on the Principles of "A Course in Miracles."* Harper Collins, 1992.

FLAVIA KATE PETERS
Newbury, Berkshire, UK

FLAVIA KATE PETERS is widely regarded as the UK's Faery advocate and has been heralded a 'leading light' in the new generation of Celestial Mediators. Flavia Kate is a natural spiritual healer and clairvoyant who offers channeled guidance, healing sessions and workshops at her 'Angel Lights' business in Newbury, Berkshire. She is regularly invited to speak at events such as at Mind Body Spirit, 3 Wishes Faery Fest and many more throughout the UK.

She is a regular columnist for Fae and Lightworker Magazines and has featured in various publications such as *Unicorn Magic* by Kitty Bishop PhD and *The Wonder of Unicorns* by Diana Cooper. Flavia Kate has appeared on TV chat shows including The Nick Ashron's Lightworker's Guide to the Galaxy, as an ambassador for the Faeries, as well as for BBC Radio, and hosts an 'Angels and Faeries' show on Radio Lightworker. Her CD *Away with the Fairies!* features visualization meditations provided by the faeries to connect people of all ages to the faery kingdom; including children, for whom she also runs faery parties and meditation groups – "keeping the magic alive."

The faeries urge us to go outside and breathe in the magic that is all around us. Take time to go barefooted on the grass, connecting us to the nourishing energy of the earth. Smell and feel the damp soil, fallen leaves, blooming flowers, tree bark, the caress of a breeze – and dance with nature!

Contact Flavia Kate and follow her events diary at www.angel-lights.co.uk

I Can See a Faery!

FLAVIA KATE PETERS

*The faeries genuinely want to help us live a healthier,
happier and more prosperous life,
for when we are harmonious with ourselves,
so too is the world directly around us.*

My very first recollection of faeries was during a hot summer's day when I was about two years old. There was a village cricket match, and I was playing with other children at the edge of the green. There stood a huge old oak tree, which had a hollow doorway at the bottom of its trunk. An older boy had a golf club that he put through the hollow and up inside of the tree. As he peered upwards he shouted "I can see a faery!"

The boy claimed that there was a small switch inside that he had knocked with the club, which turned the light on – and low and behold a faery was revealed! We all gathered around the tree desperate to see. He spent a little while turning this light switch on and off shouting "There's the faery! No she's gone. There's the faery! No she's gone." He let some of the other children take a peek up through the hollow to see his exciting new discovery. I wanted to see the faery so badly. But alas, I was left out. I guess I was too young to be chosen. When all the children eventually left, I remember peering through the hollow and up into the tree, seeing nothing but darkness. The disappointment was bitter, but what did I expect? I didn't have a golf club that could reach up to turn a faery light switch on, did I?

A year later my family moved to a house surrounded by vast woodland and there I spent my childhood peering through any hole or hollow that I could find in the trees, looking for switches that would light up the faeries. I would spend hours in the woods talking to faeries, communing with them and connecting with the nature that surrounded me. It wasn't until I was about 12 years old that I told the golf club story to a neighbor and immediately I was shot down in flames. "What utter rubbish! You are silly. There are no such things as faeries. Fancy you believing in such a thing. Didn't it even occur to you that this boy had made the whole thing up?"

Well, no it hadn't occurred to me at all. I had always felt I had a connection with faeries and I certainly believed that the boy had found that light switch in the tree. But, what if my friend was right? Of course, he must be! Oh how silly I am! I felt such a fool to have believed the story, to have believed that faeries are real! And that was the end of that. No more hunting for faeries, no more speaking to faeries – they just don't exist!

What a shame that I was ridiculed into shutting down that connection, for allowing someone else's opinion to change mine. But this is what has happened to many of us over, at least, the last one thousand years.

The faeries are the guardian angels of the plants and animals which they nurture and tend to lovingly. They are the spirits of nature, who played an important role in Celtic life in Britain before Christianity reached its shores. Back then, nature was revered by humans, daily. But when the 'new' religion swept the land, those attempting to converse with these magical beings were branded as 'evil' or a 'witch,' and were severely punished or put to death. So, sadly the faeries withdrew from human sight and sense.

The faeries made a brief comeback in the Victorian era when spiritualism was a craze and became quite fashionable, often depicted in fantasy art and oil paintings. Another reason they started to appear again was because of the Industrial Revolution – pollution filled the air, whilst land was being raped and covered with concrete and iron. The faeries needed to be seen again, so that they could share their plight and enlist human help. Now, because our planet appears to be in jeopardy, due to the destruction humans have wreaked upon it, the faeries are concerned for the welfare of the natural world, which is also part of their world. By communicating with us they hope to help us to heal the Earth.

Communicating with the faeries and recognizing the spiritual aspect of nature, as we did all those centuries ago, will help to restore balance and harmony to all; us included.

Despite having written off faeries I continued to be my spiritual self through the years, and connected very often with angels, as I have done from an early age. I was guided to California to train to become an Angel Therapist with renowned angel lady and author, Doreen Virtue PhD. The training location was stunning. The grounds were filled with the most beautiful flowers and plants that decorated pathways which led to the golden sands that lined the pacific ocean. Heaven on Earth! It was here that I was re-introduced to the faeries, one warm evening at sunset.

I was taking a stroll to the beach and felt led to smell some delicate white flowers to the left of me. Suddenly, I felt compelled to ask permission to breathe in their scent and immediately heard a small voice saying "Yes, do so." Well, I was rather surprised and stood there stunned for a moment. I heard a voice again saying "Well, will you?" So obediently I leant forward and stuck my nose in and breathed up the heavenly scent. "Thank you," I said and immediately felt something on my nose. Careful not to hurt whatever it was, I tried to gently brush it away, but continued to feel something there.

The next day in class we were asked to get into pairs. I coupled with a pretty petite lady, with long curly brown hair. She introduced herself and then exclaimed ''You have a faery on your nose. She's pink!'' So, the faeries had found their way in, and quite plainly weren't going to let me get away this time.

When I returned home, I set about building up my Angel Practice. I asked the angels to help me find a suitable place to work from and was guided to an ideal shop in my local town, which had a large spacious room at the side of the building. It was a faery shop and was run by a lady named Twinkle, who welcomed me with open arms. I was able to run angel workshops, meditation groups and give angel readings and healings comfortably. I also helped out, when I could, selling faeries items and all things sparkly.

As numbers grew I had no choice but to look for bigger premises, which didn't take long. Within days I was led to a Wellbeing Centre that had tranquil therapy rooms and the most exquisite covered courtyard, filled with plants and flowers! The place was perfect and so I signed up to continue my angel therapies from there. One day, as I was at the Center, deciding on dates

> ### Dreams Come True
>
> *The faeries wish you to know that what you have imagined is now manifesting.*
>
> *You have kept the faith with positive affirmations, visualizations and prayer, and now your dreams have moved into etheric form, ready to materialize. The faeries ask that you release any self doubt, because you truly are worthy of their help in making your fondest dreams come true!*

for more angel workshops I suddenly heard the stamping of tiny feet and voices crying, "What about us?!" It was the faeries! I felt terrible. How could I have not even thought about running faery workshops? They need to be heard; they need to be believed in!

So I consciously agreed with the faeries to be their representative. I enlisted their help so that they could give me the information that they wanted me to get across. I found that we worked very easily together. This led me to run faery events throughout the UK for adults and children alike, as well as writing articles and meditations for the faery press, and many other publications.

At one faery workshop, a slender young girl arrived who was quiet and shy and said that she didn't know why she was there, but just knew she had to be. After the first visualization meditation we did to commune with the faery kingdom, she just burst into tears. She told the group that she had always felt different, as though she didn't belong and only felt happy when she was out in nature.

I explained to her that there are many people on this planet who have been faeries in other lifetimes, who have incarnated now into human form. These brave faeries have volunteered to become human, in this lifetime, to help clean up the planet and to bring us back into commune with nature. When we are born, we go through a veil of amnesia and therefore forget, on a conscious level, who we really are. Only on a deep cellular level do we know, and that is why many incarnated faeries feel that they are different, without realizing why. They wonder why they get so angry at animals being mistreated, or when plants and crops are poisoned by chemicals, and the total disregard for the planet by humans in general.

As soon as the young faerie delegate related to this, it all made perfect sense to her. The relief and the joy of realizing who she really was and why she felt so different, was wonderful to see!

Faeries are naturally shy, and also weary of humans, so they don't often show themselves in a way that we want or expect. They are, in fact, all around us and do belong to our physical world and also their realm, Faerie Land, which is hidden within our world. It resonates at a higher energy frequency than ours – which is why it is often difficult for humans, who are of a heavier, more dense energy, to see them. But faeries can freely visit both worlds as they are made up of high vibrating energy of light. They can slow down these vibrations though, so that their bodies can take on a denser form which we are then able to see in our physical world – if we are lucky!

During another workshop, two large faeries turned up just as I was connecting the participants with the energy of a faery ring. They hovered in the air, to the right of the group who were in a meditative state with their eyes closed. Silently I asked the faeries why they were there, and they told me they just wanted to see what was 'going on.' I told them that they were welcome.

To earn one's trust, faeries will look to see if we have done unselfish deeds for the environment, such as pick up rubbish, be kind to animals and recycling. If we haven't, then they might set us tasks. Usually this is to pick up rubbish. If you walk past an empty soda can or crisp packet, or the like, and suddenly feel compelled to pick it up, you can be sure that the faeries are behind it. Go for it – because this will build up their trust and will be the start of a wonderful new relationship with the faeries. The more you follow this guidance, the more naturally it will become, until you find that you yourself are a guardian of nature. The faeries will always show you their appreciation, in some way or other – just look for the signs!

I was walking through a stretch of park that is visible to a busy town roundabout, and noticed broken green glass on the lawn that could be a potential hazard for animals, who could hurt their paws on the sharp edges. I bent down to pick up the glass pieces and took them to the nearest bin, which was quite a walk away. As I continued with this ritual, which took a good 20 minutes, I endured shouts from passing cars, and horn blowing, as if I was doing something quite mad. I just smiled, and returned no judgment. I was pleased to put the last few pieces in the bin, and as I looked toward a pretty cherry tree, what looked to me like a leprechaun-type figure appeared. He was dressed in green, including his hat, and was about 2–3 feet tall. With a knowing nod, he disappeared just as quickly as he'd arrived. I just knew that he was acknowledging what I had just done.

Faeries may not always make themselves known by appearing visually though. You may feel the presence of faeries through a change of energy, such as a feeling of euphoria or you might feel a physical push or poke. Often faeries dance on the top of people's heads. This may feel quite spidery, so be careful not to knock them off if it tickles!

They might leave you a gift, such as a stone, a crystal or even a feather (like the angels often do!) A book may jump out at you; you may overhear a relevant conversation or receive a faery-related gift from a friend.

Sometimes the faeries will send us a physical sign to acknowledge our connection with them; as they did me one brisk winter's morning:

I visited my favorite nature spot on a very sunny but cold, crisp day. There wasn't a cloud in the sky and I sat by the frozen lake surrounded by tall stark trees, on a rather cold, frosty wooden bench.

As I basked in the warmth of the sun I closed my eyes and focused on my breathing. Then, in the silence I opened my heart chakra to the nature angels. In my mind's eye I saw the faeries receiving the love that I was sending out on my exhaled breath. As I inhaled deeply I imagined breathing their love back to me, filling my heart. And so it continued for quite a while as I breathed my love out to the faeries, and breathed their love back to me in return.

When I felt ready to open my eyes, I looked up. A small light aircraft suddenly appeared and seemed to be doing acrobatics in the sky above me. Within seconds it completely vanished, but left behind a huge white fluffy HEART shape, which stood out boldly against the blue of the winter's sky.

I gasped as I realized that this was a sign in response to the connection that had just been experienced. The faeries had sent me a sign to acknowledge that the love felt was very real. I knew instantly in that moment with their LOVE and support, anything is possible!

The faeries genuinely want to help us live a healthier, happier and more prosperous life, for when we are harmonious with ourselves, so too is the world directly around us. Faeries can work as our helpers and guides on our spiritual pathway and with any aspect of our lives. All we need to do is just ask. The faeries will help in lots of ways – and often not in the way that we expect. So once we've requested their help, we should allow the faeries to get to work without interfering.

Faeries can assist us with material concerns. They are brilliant manifestors, meaning they know how to attract or create dreams and make them a reality, for this is what they do naturally. They remind us of the importance of staying focused on, and positive about, our desires.

If you need your financial life healed, or an abundant flow of prosperity, for instance, then you can count your lucky stars that you are friends with the faeries. All they do is imagine what they want and it is created for them in an instant. For example, they may picture themselves with a big cream cake – and hey presto, a big cream cake appears! The fairies tell us that we actually do the same. Whatever we think transforms into reality in the ethers. Then it is through asking for assistance, and then taking guided action that we can bring, with the faeries' help, our dreams into reality.

I was given this exact information during a healing session, as I was guided to see, in my mind's eye, the client's ailment as perfectly whole and healed. I realized that this was how the faeries live and bring about all that they desire, and decided to work with them in this way.

I had been invited to attend a faery ball in Cornwall, which was about a 5 hour drive from where I lived. I longed to go and join in such fun! Having a lean month I was concerned about paying for accommodation and the cost of fuel to travel. So, I visualized it all as happening and asked the faeries to assist in my desire. I then felt guided to buy a lotto scratch card (which I don't ever usually do!) But the feeling was so strong, that I went ahead and choose 'Lucky Leprechaun.' Back at home I was putting the key into the lock of my front door and heard the words, "You shall go to the ball." I raced inside and lit a small faery candle and sat crossed legged in front of it, the words still echoing through my mind. With a coin I carefully scratched off the silver coating, to reveal three green shamrocks! I had won a hundred pounds!! That would pay for petrol and food for my trip away. How wonderful. But what of accommodation? With that, a text message appeared on my mobile phone, from a friend, inviting me to stay for that time in a delightful cottage overlooking the Cornish coast with no charge!

As the faeries had proven to me, this is a very powerful way to create our lives. Remember to be careful what you are imagining, as the faeries have access to what we are seeing in our minds. Sometimes it's fun to play with the faeries in this way – for example, you could imagine yourself with very pointy pixie ears and a long, long nose and it is 'real' in the ethers, instantly. The faeries can see this and will laugh! It's a great way to build up a relationship with the faeries for they enjoy laughter and playing with the magical energies that are all around us. So because of the faeries' magical abilities to create what they desire, we too can call upon the faeries to assist us!

If you, and they, feel that you have a good relationship with them, then the faeries will immediately set to work to bring you what you desire (for the highest good of all, of course). All you have to do is be clear about what you want and ask – and remember the phrase "be careful what you wish for!" – remembering that whatever you are imagining, the faeries have access to.

Now at this critical time on the planet the faeries urge us to be their voice; they are calling us to be the ambassadors of nature and help heal and clean up this beautiful planet. In return they will easily supply us with our material needs so that we have the peace to focus on the mission before us.

The faeries are waiting to share with us the magic that exists within and all around us. They reveal the beauty and power of our inner-selves and can assist us with magical solutions and insights to situations.

All we need to do is BELIEVE!

Meditation to Connect with the Faery Realm

We can connect with the faeries at anytime, especially when we are relaxed or out in nature. So invite the faeries in, and allow them to help you to shine . . .

Find a quiet spot where you won't be disturbed – preferably outside, or next to a plant or crystal. Breathing steadily – in and out – see yourself surrounded by an iridescent ball of rainbow light, which protects you fully with angel energy. With your eyes closed, take three deep breaths – inhale and release, inhale and release, inhale and release – and now let your breath remain deep, but steady.

As you continue to breathe, you begin to sense a smell – something quite familiar – what is it? You know this scent; you recognize it – but can't quite grasp it. You know it is from memories long, long ago. Something comforting, safe, but also wonderful – something that you connect with at the deepest level. And then in your mind's eye you find that you are sitting against a huge, strong tree in a grassy glade. Your back leans against the rough bark and you feel the spongy green moss beneath you. You can hear the beautiful song of birds . . .

As you look around, you see mighty, majestic trees surrounding the glade – see the bright green of their leaves as the sunlight streams through them. It is beautiful and you notice that as these shafts of bright golden light shine through the trees, they meet together, as one blast of blinding light, in the clearing just in front of you.

Your eyes squint at the brightness, but you cannot take your eyes off this sight – it's like nature's own treasure chest of gold!

The light is getting larger and brighter and expands out, getting nearer and nearer to you – and you feel more and more comforted, more and more at peace and you just know that this is the light of the Divine, the light of the Mother coming to nurture you and to fill you with her goodness.

Breathe in the light . . . feel it fill your heart . . . feel your heart expand like a flower opening . . . breathing this pure light energy in, as it fills your body – all the way down through the legs, into the feet and out of the soles of your feet, into the ground, deep into the Earth . . . And you instantly feel a connection with the energy of the Earth, the Earth magic mixing with the light that is now within you and part of you.

Breathe this new energy up – the mixture of earth energy and your own Divine light. Feel it as you draw it up in through your feet, up your legs – feel the surge as it rushes to fill your entire body, breathe it in as this amazing light cleanses every cell, every vessel . . . moving on up through the throat, moving through your face, filling your head and bursting out of your crown at the top your head – up and up – reaching to the highest levels of love . . .

Feel and see the light expanding outwards – showering down over and around you . . . this beautiful light of protection, love and magic energy – filling you, surrounding you and connecting you with below and above. Bathe in this glorious light, soaking in the Divine energy – feeling every part of you coming alive.

As the sun moves round, the shafts of light become hidden from the trees and your eyes adjust slowly. You are beginning to see the woodland that you are sitting in.

Just there you see some movement, a spark of light – no, two or three – no more, many more . . . sparkling orbs, dancing in and out of the trees – and with a rub of your eyes, you see in front of you 'tiny' folk – yes faeries! But 'oh' also elves and other beings who have come to greet you! So many of them, all approaching – some smiling and some looking very shy – and you realize that you are sitting in the heart of the faeries' ring!

Take some time to be introduced and then introduce yourself. Open your heart, so that they know they can trust you. Find out what these magical beings have come to tell you – what do they want you to know? What would you like to tell them? What would you like their help with? Listen well to their response on all levels.

One of your new friends whispers their name and another puts something in your hand.

Dusk is falling, and you feel a chill – it is time for you to come back and so you say your goodbyes. You feel such joy, such amazement that you have just connected with the Faerie Realm; you have been chosen as a faerie confident and you know that you can connect with these new friends any time, for they will always be there for you.

But how are you able to leave this place of magic and wonder? And then it comes to you, quite clearly . . . you breathe . . . deeply . . . taking a deep inhale and exhale, inhale and exhale, inhale . . . and gently open your eyes.

Welcome back!

❧

Taken from *Away with the Fairies!* meditation CD © Flavia Kate Peters 2009.

Nature

*Your angels encourage you to open
your heart to the magic of Nature.*

*Spend some time enjoying the
tranquility of Nature. Nature's angels,
the animals and Nature Spirits, have
important messages for you, to help
you more easily discover and nurture
your hidden gifts and talents.*

SOPHIA FAIRCHILD
Sydney, Australia

SOPHIA FAIRCHILD is an international author, editor, writing coach, spiritual teacher and publisher, currently living on the beautiful Sydney Harbour foreshore.

She is a certified Soul Coach®, Past Life Therapist, Gateway Dreaming™ and Space Clearing practitioner, personally trained by the remarkable Denise Linn. Sophia is also an Angel Therapist®, certified by Doreen Virtue PhD, and a Faery Intuitive.

Sophia grew up around Australian aboriginal people, saw faeries and spoke to angels and spirits as a child. Her Irish great aunts and Aboriginal great grandfather profoundly influenced her intuitive gifts, playfulness and love of storytelling.

Both a seasoned writer and award-winning editor, Sophia's stories have appeared in many publications, including *Soul Moments*, also published as *Coincidence or Destiny*, edited by Phil Cousineau, foreword by Robert A. Johnson, Conari Press, 1997; *Traveler's Tales: Tuscany*, Traveler's Tales Guides, 2001; *Angels 101*, by Doreen Virtue, Hay House, 2006; *Angel on My Shoulder*, Malachite Press, 2007; *The Miracles of Archangel Michael*, by Doreen Virtue, Hay House, 2008; *Soul Whispers, Collective Wisdom from Soul Coaches around the World*, Soul Wings® Press, 2009; *The Healing Miracles of Archangel Raphael*, by Doreen Virtue, Hay House, 2010; *Soul Whispers II: Secret Alchemy of the Elements in Soul Coaching*, Soul Wings® Press, 2011, and *The Wisdom We Have Gained*, edited by Kim Pentecost.

Look for the next book edited by Sophia Fairchild ~ *Planet Whispers: Wisdom from Soul Travelers around the World* in 2011.

For editing and publishing services contact Sophia at Soul Wings® Press.

www.SoulWingsPress.com

Archangels and Nature Angels

SOPHIA FAIRCHILD

The whispers of angels can be heard in many forms. The following three stories show how contact with the angelic realm can be made not only through angels, but through animals and faeries as well!

The Hero

When the cat stared directly into my eyes,
I instantly knew he was warning me of danger.

It was a peaceful Sunday afternoon, late one rainy Southern California winter, yet the day was so warm I'd spent hours in the garden in my bikini, reading and tending to my flowers. Noticeably absent was the neighbor's cat, who always climbed over the fence to join me whenever he heard me tinkering about in the back garden.

This cat was a large, mixed-breed male who, though de-sexed, behaved like a Tom. He had a grumpy, authoritative air, was highly territorial and had a nasty habit of biting anyone who tried to pet him. And yet, he loved to curl up by my side, purring, whenever I sat in the warm sunshine to meditate. Later, when his owners returned, I'd watch his muscular body clambering up over my wooden fence on his way home for dinner. Sometimes he would pause on top of the high side gate, looking back as if to remind me to get this gate fixed. It would often get stuck in a closed position after rain.

It was the day of the Academy Awards in Hollywood, and I was planning to watch the early arrivals on the red carpet live on TV later that afternoon. After several blissful hours in the garden, I began preparing a delicious vegetable pie to later enjoy while watching the movie stars showing off their glittering finery as they arrived for the evening's celebrations. My house was clean and tidy, and there was enough time to take a nice long bubble bath before settling in for an evening of light entertainment watching the Oscars.

Just as I was about to run my bath water, I heard a faint muttering sound outside my kitchen door. It sounded like a man's voice. I assumed it was someone talking on their cell phone in front of my house, so I ignored it. But suddenly, my neighbor's big cat came running through my open back door, straight into the kitchen. He jumped up onto a counter beside the kitchen door, which led out onto my driveway. The cat began arching his back and hissing at someone or something that I couldn't see, on the other side of that door.

This was very strange behavior for this cat, so I crept forward to see if I could make out the words that I could still hear being faintly muttered on the other side of that door. I saw the shadow of a man standing there, just as he began to knock on the door. The mumbled words I heard were chilling! He was saying that he had a knife, and that he was going to break down the door unless I opened it. What was even more terrifying was that he was speaking softly enough not to be overheard by my neighbors.

The neighbor's cat arched his back and fluffed up his tail, looking like a tiger as he crouched in an attack position on my kitchen counter. When the cat stared directly into my eyes, I instantly knew he was warning me of danger. I clearly heard these words in my mind "Run! Run for your life!" I stood frozen for a moment, barefoot in my bikini, there in my fragrant kitchen, where a moment ago everything had been a scene of perfect tranquility. Suddenly, the cat screeched and leapt off the counter, then flew through the house and out the back door. I grabbed the first piece of clothing I could see, scooped up my garden flip-flops and raced out the back door into the garden, right on the heels of my neighbor's cat.

Just when we'd reached the safety of the garden, I heard the sickening crash of my kitchen door being broken down, along with the sound of shattering glass. My heart was in my mouth as I struggled to open the tall side gate to escape to the other side of the house. But the gate was stuck! The cat had already disappeared over the fence but the fence and gate were both too high for me to climb. I threw on the dress I was holding in my hand, slipped on the flip flops, then tried again with all my might to force that gate open, all the while thinking the intruder must be right behind me.

I silently called to my angels for help. Somehow, with superhuman strength, I managed to fling open the jammed gate and take cover in the shrubs along the opposite side of the house. By now I could hear the intruder moving around inside my home looking for me. I had to escape before he found me! Not knowing whether he could see me or not, I made a desperate dash across the open front garden, then leapt over the front fence, down a sheer drop of six feet and onto the pavement below. I ran next door to the neighbor's house to call for help. But they weren't home! A passerby saw me and asked if something was wrong. I told him there was a man inside my house and that he'd broken down my side door. He said he'd call the police and told me to run away across the street to safety. As soon as my neighbors opposite welcomed me into their home, they let me telephone the police. Standing there gasping for breath on the phone, I noticed that I had put my dress on inside out.

I then watched mesmerized with my neighbors as a squadron of police vehicles converged on my house, the intruder still inside. A heavily armed tactical response team in black, bullet-proof armor crept up both sides of my house, hiding in the bushes just as I had done earlier. The police dispatcher kept me on the phone, relaying questions to me from the officer in charge on the scene and keeping me updated on their progress. The S.W.A.T. Team continued to move stealthily around my garden until they had secured the perimeter of the property.

It was just like watching a movie, only it was real! The whole street was blocked during the siege, which dragged on for several hours. All the while, I prayed that the intruder would not be shot inside my home and that the cat was safe. Finally, after a long and tense standoff, we watched as a police negotiator convinced the man to surrender and come outside with his hands up. As soon as he stepped out my front door, five huge police officers jumped on top of him, threw him on his stomach and cuffed his hands behind his back, right there on my front lawn.

The Academy Awards must be the longest show on television. So, when I was finally allowed back inside my own home after the forensics team had finished going over it, I still managed to see the last few moments of the delayed broadcast. Later, the local media wanted to interview me about the home invasion, calling me a hero. This seemed completely absurd, and I told them so.

All along I had known that the real hero was the neighbor's grumpy cat, who arrived just in time to warn me that I was in danger, just like a guardian angel. Had he not been there, I would probably have opened my door to that crazed stranger, and might not be here to tell this story now.

Epilogue: I later learned that this violent intruder was mentally ill and high on the wrong prescription drugs at the time. Apparently after driving from another city, he had mistaken my house for one of his relative's. In the months that followed, I worked with the Parole Board to get him the treatment he needed and to have his jail time reduced in exchange for sober service to the community.

Archangel in Ireland

*Instead of using our own energy to heal, we need to step out of the way
and allow the greater powers of healing to flow through us.*

I had called upon Archangel Raphael in the past to assist myself and others whenever healing was needed. But it wasn't until I found myself in the lunar-like landscape of the Burren, in the West of Ireland, that I really felt the full force of Archangel Raphael's powerful healing abilities.

The Burren is a 100-square-mile plateau of limestone rock that looks very much like the surface of the moon. This mystical landscape contains dozens of Celtic crosses, ancient fortresses and megalithic tombs. Though its surface appears smooth, the Burren is full of dangerous potholes out of which grow the rarest of plants. Yet there are no trees of any kind for as far as the eye can see.

Our small group of travelers had carefully made its way across this wide moonlike plateau to set stones on a sacred pile of rocks, leaving our prayers the way travelers do in the Himalayas. The cold wind howled across the open plain, making us shiver in the summer sun, so most of our group had already turned back for shelter. I placed my small stone on the cairn and turned to leave. Just then, I watched with horror as a middle-aged man slipped and fell awkwardly into one of the deep potholes under our feet.

He lay there, unable to move, obviously in great pain. Shouts for help went unanswered as the fierce wind swept all sound away. The man groaned and began lapsing into shock. We were in the middle of nowhere with no help of any kind. As his wife ran back across the plateau to seek assistance, I found myself alone with an injured stranger, somewhere in the west country of Ireland, on the wild, windswept plains of the Burren.

I knew I must stay with him and offer some kind of assistance, but had no idea what to do. The injured man was a German doctor who spoke little English. I was someone with no medical training who'd never done any kind of direct healing before, and spoke no German. He pointed to his hip and said, "Kaput," meaning that it was broken. Not knowing what else to do, I gently placed my hand on his leg and began praying that healing energy would flow though me to him.

Archangel Raphael

The Archangel of healing is with you now; be open to receiving his support.

A miraculous power surrounds you now which, when directed through your heart, mind or hands can be extremely beneficial in many different ways. The key to this powerful, healing energy is love.

As soon as I did this, I felt the presence of Archangel Raphael with us. I could feel the angel sending powerful, green healing light to the site of the injury, and was surprised to find myself the conduit for this concentrated flow of healing.

I didn't so much *see* this energy as the color green; rather, I *felt* the color green surrounding the archangel's presence. His aura felt like the soft, refreshing atmosphere of a cool waterfall in a lush, green rainforest. It was as if a fountain of vitalizing healing force was being poured down upon us, funneling into the body of the man lying on the rocks.

At first, it was my own energy that had flowed through my hand into the injured man's leg. But with Archangel Raphael's intervention, the healing force flowing through me was now coming directly from the angel.

I smiled at the German doctor, and he smiled back at me in silence. He too could feel the comforting presence of the angel as he drifted in and out of consciousness. After what seemed like an age, the doctor's wife returned with a blanket, saying that a rescue team was on its way. She gave me a hug and told me it was alright to leave them now, that all was well. I later heard that her husband was flown back to Germany that same day and recovered rapidly after emergency surgery.

It was only after this experience that I began to train as a healer. Archangel Raphael had demonstrated to me that instead of using our own energy to heal, we need to step out of the way and allow the greater powers of healing to flow through us. This not only prevents us from becoming depleted, but ensures that the energy being sent to the other person is of the highest vibration.

Since that time, I have worked even more closely with Archangel Raphael, who is also a wonderful traveling companion!

The Angel Plant

Faeries are most often found in secluded and mysterious places,
so it was truly a blessing to be able to connect with them
at the appointed secret spots.

Archangel Ariel visited me during the summer I joined a local community garden project in Sydney. I was so excited about being able to grow fresh organic vegetables to share with my neighbors, right in the heart of our large city!

Earlier that summer, a potted plant was gifted to me by a neighbor who was moving away and couldn't take this nameless plant with her. Though it looked like an ordinary house plant, it contained a very strong presence. The plant appeared tired and stressed, so I placed it in a cool position inside my home, under a painting of the Goddess of Spring, to allow it time to rest. Then, suddenly, in mid summer, the mystery plant began to bloom.

I'd never seen a plant like this in flower before, and was amazed at the delicacy of its tiny white blossoms. Their sweet, hypnotic fragrance wafted through every room of my home like a blessing. It was this intense fragrance that greeted me first thing each morning upon awakening. The beauty of its perfume was such that I often woke with tears of joy in my eyes, filled with gratitude for the amazing gift of this once-abandoned plant, which by now I had named "The Angel Plant."

One morning, just after the Angel Plant began to magically bloom, Archangel Ariel swept into my life in a great whoosh of pinkish-gold white light. Her powerful presence filled the rooms of my home, just like the heady scent of the magical Angel Plant.

At the time, I was preparing to teach a faery workshop in the nearby parklands. Archangel Ariel instantly ignited a fiery muse in my heart. I felt a great wave of inspiration radiating towards me. Ariel filled my mind with a long list of topics on teaching about the water element and the faery realm, the ideas flowing so fast, I could barely keep up as I tried to jot them down.

The angel urged me to go immediately to the parklands where I was to teach my faery workshop. She had something she wanted to show me. I pulled on my comfortable shoes and strode the two blocks to the park. As I meandered through its tree-lined trails, Ariel introduced me to faery beings who wished to assist me with the various ideas she had suggested.

As we proceeded, I was shown a magical faery walk along which to lead my workshop participants. This would help them to connect with the Spirit of Water, as well as the Nature Spirits who oversee the water element. I was then led directly to a secret spring, hidden beneath wild, overgrown bushes, deep inside a small forest. I immediately sensed the clarity of this pure water source as it bubbled up from deep within the holy earth. Archangel Ariel asked me to bless this spring and to honor it each time I came to this park. I was shown several other vantage points from which to bless the lakes and streams of the parklands, and much more.

After this first adventure with Ariel in the park, several nature angels came home with me to assist in my projects. Each day I sat in my courtyard garden to meditate with them. Before long, they had given me the formula, and specific instructions, on how to make a flower essence and aura spray from a particularly beautiful plant blooming in my summer garden. They called this essence "I See Faeries!" I dutifully followed their directions to create the formula, which included specific essential oils and gemstone elixirs. All of this occurred during the week of a summer full moon.

As soon as I'd completed the faery spray, Archangel Ariel gave me a formula for a new magical blend. I was to create this from the blossoms of the magnificent Angel Plant which was still enfolding my home in a blanket of divine fragrance. I wasn't to know until later that the Angel Plant only blooms for two weeks each year. It was within those two weeks that I made up the mother tincture for the angel aura spray called "I See Angels!" based on Ariel's specific directions. It still astonishes me that these two magical blends can be so powerful, yet so gentle. Thanks to Archangel Ariel, people who've used them report healing properties beyond anything I had envisioned.

On the day of the faery workshop, I led our joyful group in exactly the way Archangel Ariel and the faeries had suggested, sending blessings not only to all the water sources, but to all the water birds, the earth and the trees, all the other wildlife, and in particular, to the nature spirits who watch over them all. Faeries are most often found in secluded and mysterious places, so it was truly a blessing to be able to connect with them at the appointed secret spots.

There had been an ongoing drought for a number of years prior to this, but on the day of the workshop, the dawn broke to a glorious sunny day, following several days of torrential rain! All of the streams and lakes in the park were now overflowing with crystal clear rainwater. The sacred spring which Ariel had shown me was now hidden beneath a brand new lake! We all sent a blessing to this amazing body of water, which now combined waters from the ancient underground spring, together with pure raindrops from the sky. This magical lake lasted only a day, before draining away naturally.

In her wisdom, Archangel Ariel had demonstrated the truth that sacred things can be beautiful but rare, like this magical lake, and just like the delicate white flowers of the Angel Plant, which only blooms for two weeks each year.

Meditation to Meet your Faery Guide

Move into a comfortable position and begin to relax, taking in some deep breaths.

Place your hands gently in your lap, and allow all tension to be released, as you exhale . . .

Breathe in light with every breath . . .

We call upon the mighty archangels, ascended masters, your angels and faery guardians, your guides and your ancestors, to come forth to create a very loving and safe circle around you . . . so that you can step easily into this journey with a deep sense of safety and joy.

Feel the archangels' presence around you now, as you continue to breathe in and out, allowing yourself to relax and simply breathe . . .

On this journey, you will meet with your faery guide and travel together, back in time, to those mystical shores . . . to the magic and wisdom of Avalon.

As you continue to breathe, all tension is leaving your body. You feel pleasantly relaxed.

Now, imagine yourself in a beautiful, sunny place in Nature. This is a place of sanctuary for you, a quiet, peaceful place, where you feel completely safe, happy and at ease.

Imagine the singing of birds or the sound of water. Smell the plants and trees nearby. Feel the gentle touch of the breeze on your skin and hair. Feel the ground beneath your feet.

Here in this beautiful place, you feel a sense of joy. You are completely at peace, and know that you are completely safe.

And high above you there is a light . . . Floating down . . .

This light, coming down from above . . . is getting bigger and brighter . . .

Oh! It's a large faery! A beautiful faery . . . with wings!!

This is your faery guide, standing right in front of you!

You feel the gentle, wise energy of your faery guide, greeting you with immense compassion and love . . .

Your faery guide has always been with you, and knows everything about you.

As you step forward, faery wings of rainbow light enfold you, holding you, embracing you. You feel very safe, and very loved.

Your faery guide is willing to accompany you on a magical journey . . .

Imagine now that you are standing on the edge of a deep lake in the hush of twilight . . . A deep mist is covering the water, and you cannot see more than a few feet in front of you.

You become aware of a gentle splashing sound . . . Slowly, a majestic barge glides into view. It floats silently across the water towards you, and comes to rest on the shore. Notice the intricate carvings on this boat and its billowing sail. You now step into this barge with your faery guide, and come to rest on silken pillows.

Your barge begins to move softly through the heavy mists shrouding everything . . .

This boat is carrying you across a magical lake, allowing you to travel back through time and space, to the mystical shores of Avalon . . .

You begin to feel a sense of 'remembering'... of 'coming home'... as you drift across this calm lake... closer and closer to the shores of Avalon...

And now the mists begin to lift. You have reached the shores of Avalon.

Your magical barge comes to rest on a small beach, and you step ashore to find yourself on an enchanted island... the Isle of Avalon, on a warm spring day!

You begin to walk through the apple orchards of Avalon, smelling the fresh fragrance of fruit and noticing tiny apple blossoms floating down, creating a snowy white carpet beneath the trees...

You can still feel your faery guide's presence behind you, as you find yourself moving through beautiful gardens, filled with flowers and plants...

Birds are singing in the trees and colorful butterflies flit through the warm sunlight.

Suddenly you find yourself being greeted by a mysterious woman.

She is the Queen of this magical realm and she bids you welcome!

You may stay here for a while to speak with her... She has the gift of the Second Sight and is talented in the ancient arts. She knows how to work with healing herbs, colored stones and symbols, and she may share some of those secrets with you.

And now you notice, as you too begin to see with your Second Sight... that you and the garden and every plant and tree are completely surrounded by a host of small faeries!

Take a few moments to drink in your surroundings here on the Isle of Avalon.

Notice everything you are seeing and experiencing...

You remember now what it feels like to be completely at home and at peace.

But now, your faery guide reminds you that it is time to go. You bow with gratitude to the Lady and take your leave, knowing that you can return here again at any time in the future. As you say farewell to Avalon, you feel joy in your heart, having visited this magical place of myth and legend!

And now, your faery guide leads you back down to the beautiful barge, and you float gently back the way you came, through the mists... across the magical lake.

As you reach the other side of the lake, arriving back where you began in your beautiful, sunny place in Nature, your faery guide reaches out to give you something.

It is a gift for you, to remind you of this journey.

It is also a gift that carries the energy of Avalon, something you can use in your present life.

You can either carry this gift with you, or place it inside your heart.

Know that you will carry this gift with you always.

Now the time has come for you to say farewell to your faery guide. But you know that you can call on your guide at any time for assistance. Your faery guide embraces you, brushing you gently with gossamer wings, and you feel the depth of this being's unconditional love for you.

Having now said your fond farewells to your faery guide, you turn to walk back through your beautiful place in Nature, knowing that you will always carry the peace and beauty of Avalon in your heart.

Now see yourself for a moment, being showered with a sparkling, cleansing energy from above. Feel the crisp, tingling essence of this cleansing shower . . .

Allow your energy to go back down into Mother Earth, feeling the fresh green richness of her soil. Now pull your energy back up through your chakras, up to your heart chakra.

And now you are returning to your normal waking reality, into the present time and place, feeling fully refreshed and alive, your heart filled with joy and gratitude.

And so it is . . .

∽

DENISE BURANT
Saskatchewan, Canada

DENISE IS AN Angel Therapy Practitioner® certified by Dr. Doreen Virtue. She is also certified in Past Life Regression Healing and Level 1 Reiki. Her practice is focused upon animal communication with the intention of healing pets and their owners equally. Denise works with the angels and incorporates Reiki energy during sessions. She also offers Angel Readings and Past Life Healings.

While working full time in Health Care, Denise also works with a local pet rescue group called People for Animals of Saskatchewan Inc. She provides foster home care to several cats at any given time which in turn offers her daily opportunities to practice animal healing and communication. Denise feeds feral cats from a feeding station in her backyard daily and offers them Reiki treatments and healings.

Together with a fellow Angel Therapy Practitioner, Denise has designed and teaches Past Life Regression Healing Workshops. Two levels of Angel Kid's Camps have been developed out of a need that was identified at the first PLR class and were first offered in the summer of 2010. Denise also developed an angel-themed bingo game for these children's camps along with special angel information cards on angels, fairies and power animals.

Meditation CDs on Past Life Regression and Animal Healing & Communication have been developed, produced and are in circulation. For further information on Denise's workshops on Animal Healing & Communication and Meeting your Power Animals, contact Denise at www.wingsofhealing.ca or wingsofhealing@sasktel.net.

Rusty's memoriam can be read at: http://www.people4animals.ca/index.php?docID=145&searchtext=rusty

Wings of Healing

DENISE BURANT

*Rusty not only showed me that anything is possible when one loves enough,
but that communication and healing work both ways.*

I knew that 2009 was going to hold a lot of changes for me. Little did I know
that it would be life altering. That spring I decided to move forward with my
angel work and started by taking Dr. Doreen Virtue's Angel Therapy Practitioner
course in June. After signing up I was excited for the day to come when I would
head off to Kona, Hawaii with my friend for my ATP Certification.

For several months prior I had been considering becoming a foster carer for
cats. I prepared my own two cats, Kiji and Raja, by having them vaccinated
appropriately and considering how they would feel having multiple other cats in
the home. In March 2009 I saw a plea by one of the pet rescuers through People
for Animals, and that is how it all began. I started with one little black female cat
and within a couple of days I had a momma cat and her litter of kittens. By mid
May all of the foster cats had been adopted out and I was looking forward to my
Kona adventure.

On Friday, May 8th, I received the call that would change my life. The same pet
rescuer said they had found a cat in a ditch in very dire straits. He probably only
had hours to live when he was discovered. She said that he had been vet checked
and felt he would be a good match for my home. They called him Rusty. I said
I would take him in but he would need somewhere to go by June 3rd as I was
leaving June 4th for Hawaii.

Rusty was a handsome six-year-old tabby and white male cat. He had the most
beautiful green/gold eyes but he was dehydrated, matted, dirty and very weak. His
body weight should have been around eight pounds but he barely weighed four. He
had difficulty standing on his two back legs and kind of shimmied along on his
belly and two front paws, trying to get his back legs to work properly. In fact he was
so emaciated that just touching him caused him obvious pain. He badly needed a
bath and brushing, but before that, love. Rusty showed his spunk right away and
gave me a head butt like I have never had before. Yes, the guy definitely had spunk.
A head butt from a cat is a way of them showing love and asking for love in return.
He gave me his story in a loud voice telling me all about his journey. When I tried

to pet him, he bit me because of the pain to his poor body with its jutting bones. But he was a very talkative guy and had no trouble showing me what he wanted!

The first night I spent hand-feeding him kitten food every hour. His poor stomach was so shrunken from not eating that he could only tolerate small meals. By the end of the second day I was able to give him a bath and a brushing, and pulled off a tick from his neck. He didn't like the smell of the other cats and would growl, chuff and try to eat all at once. Rusty also showed me he had a sense of humor. At this point I was well trained in hand feeding, but was beginning to think this might not be a good idea for a future adopter. The following day he was already showing improvement with proper nutrition and hydration. Rusty was a trooper and started using his back legs more to scratch at boxes and walk around his room. His bowels had to be dealt with as well since he had some very loose movements which could cause dehydration.

Rusty continued to improve into the next day. He was able to jump onto my bed though he was very stiff and sore. He desperately wanted to be cuddled and held but it was just too painful for him. The poor boy couldn't lie down on his side for very long. If I tried to pet him he would attack my hand as if to say, "Stop that, it hurts!" He loved to follow me around the house but was cautious around the other cats. He probably couldn't defend himself and so was a bit afraid of them. Rusty would nip my shin when he wanted attention or give me a head butt if that was an option. I could already tell that he would be a cuddle bug once his body healed itself.

At this point I was thinking the guy should have a name more suited to his ability to survive against all odds and illustrate his strong will to live. When I went to work on the Monday, Rusty was asleep on my bed in the sun, finally able to relax. He was starting to look as if he was filling out, although I did have some concerns about his kidneys, and his hips looked sunken in. I could kiss and touch his head and shoulders all I wanted to, but his back end was off limits. The moment I started to pet him at the back of his body he would nip at my hand or cry out plaintively. But he became comfortable with my two cats and they each settled into their corners of the home.

By day five, Rusty was able to clean himself which was a big deal as it indicated he was getting flexibility back in his limbs. Rusty liked to wake me up at 4:00 am for his first breakfast by head butting me until I woke up. Once he was fed I was able to go back to bed until I actually had to get up for work. Then it was time for his second breakfast. Rusty's days were filled with relaxing in the sun, eating, and of course healing. It was a big moment when his litter box could be moved to the basement as it meant he could handle stairs.

Friday, May 15th was noted as a special day as Rusty jumped onto my bed, lay down beside me, and started head butting me to be petted. As I was petting him he leaned over and started kissing my nose, real kisses with his mouth, not licking it. I remember thinking, "It doesn't get any better than this."

Each day he improved was a milestone, as he was able to perform simple tasks by himself and with less effort, from being able to jump on a bed, balancing in a litter box without shaking, to playing. He would now let me scratch his tummy which was very ticklish and his coat was becoming shiny and soft. Rusty was a toucher and when he was being petted he would reach out with his paws and touch your face or hair. Rusty showed me immediately that he was all about love. He had a very big heart. It was getting closer to the time I was to leave for Hawaii and I knew there was no other place for Rusty than my home. So I hired a pet sitter to live in my house while I was away.

The course in Hawaii was wonderful and I returned ready to follow my angel work path. It was with surprise that I arrived home to discover that Rusty wasn't doing so well. Once again he needed to be nursed back to health. He was eating and eliminating excessively which needed to be dealt with. But true to his nature and his spunk, Rusty pulled himself through and he was once again on the road to good health. He was doing so well that we got him vaccinated and put him up for adoption. Rusty was close to the weight a cat his size should be and he was looking far different from the cat that was rescued from a ditch in the spring. It was a banner moment.

Then, things went awry. Rusty started to lose weight and be sickly again. I brought in an animal healer who said that he wanted to live and was willing to fight. This was good news to me and I was willing to do whatever it took to help him win that fight. His adoption ad was pulled and he was taken back and forth to the vet for various tests. Late one Saturday, the test results were revealed. Rusty was diabetic. By vaccinating him without knowing he was diabetic we had caused him to get ill. One of the wonderful pet rescuers from People for Animals arranged the medications and together we gave Rusty the subcutaneous fluids and insulin he needed to get him through to Monday when he would return to the vet for a couple of days of intensive treatment. I learned how to give him insulin shots twice a day, test his glucose levels using a monitor and test his urine, but watched as my beautiful boy sunk lower and lower. It was not a great weekend. By Monday I couldn't wait for the vet clinic to open up so I could get the little guy in.

Rusty went to the vet clinic to spend the night where he was put on IV fluids while his glucose levels were tested regularly that day. We realized that somehow through a miscommunication he had been given ten times the amount of insulin he should have been receiving. That evening I went to see him at the clinic and told him that if he wanted to go home to the angels I would miss him but I didn't want him to suffer. I held him for awhile and left the vet clinic in tears. Well, once again Rusty proved how strong his will to live was and rallied back. On Tuesday I brought him home and was more than willing to continue to try to bring this handsome fellow back to health. Rusty never lost his ability to show love. Each night he would sleep on my pillow with his face against mine or his nose in my ear purring loudly. This didn't help me sleep but how could one ask him to stop?

I spent my summer holidays trying to bring this guy back to where he had been before. He would gain weight, and then lose it. He was eating a lot but eliminating a lot as well. People were feeling bad about not recognizing the situation or diagnosing the diabetes based on the eating and elimination signs I had been observing and mentioning. Over the next few weeks Rusty's insulin was adjusted, his food was monitored and his blood and urine were tested. I had been telling people diabetes was not something I wanted to deal with. I had worked with injured animals, but never one that was chronically ill, and diabetes was something I was nervous about dealing with. During this time I was also trying to get my basement renovated so I could have an angel room to do my angel therapy in.

In doing a reading I received the message that Rusty had a strong tie to the other side. A fellow Angel Therapy Practitioner friend of mine saw him with a halo over his head, wearing a crystal collar. I did not want to hear that. I spent that summer in tears a lot of the time. I remember Rusty would sit on the computer desk in front of me and stroke my face with his paw. I would be crying and apologizing for letting him down and he would be stroking my face as if to say, "It's OK, everything is as it should be."

Once again Rusty showed what a fighter he truly was. By September he had rallied back from near death again and was on the road to recovery. I had researched feline diabetes and I was ready to help him fight this disease. I read numerous online sites and I consulted with a local pet nutritionist. I was elated to hear that feline diabetes can be beaten if caught soon enough, and if the cat is fed the proper diet. He still had to regain the weight as he was back to square one and was in a fragile state. I was able to take him outside in my secure back yard where he would lie on the grass in the sun enjoying the afternoon. He even tried to catch a bird though, in reality, there was no way that was going to happen. Rusty was becoming known as an inspiration to the People for Animals group.

I should say I would have adopted Rusty myself but he and Kiji, my own cat, just did not get along. In fact he tormented her, so I knew I had to find him another 'forever' home.

In October my friend and I decided to take the Past Life Regression class in Kona with Dr. Doreen Virtue. I wasn't going to take any chances with Rusty's health and booked him into the vet clinic to be boarded while I was away. I remember a scene a few days before I left where I looked over my shoulder to see Kiji sitting on the toilet seat with Rusty on the floor beneath her. They had finally made their peace. I decided that adopting Rusty upon my return was now a possibility. Sitting on the cool linoleum floor of the bathroom was Rusty's favorite spot. I took him to the vet on the day I was leaving, complete with his own suitcase of medications, syringes, food, favorite blanket and litter. I left instructions that no heroic measures were to be taken. If Rusty crashed while I was away, they were to let him go home in peace.

My friend and I had an amazing experience in Kona. On the way back I was given a message by the angels to teach a class with my friend and a musician that we are both friends with. I made copious notes during the cab ride to the airport and was excited about getting home to start moving forward with my angel business. I was antsy all the way home, kind of impatient in security queues, wanting things to get moving more quickly. There were delays at every airport and we were over an hour late getting home.

Our friendly musician was there to greet us at the airport and drive us home. I wanted to get home, go to the vet, pick up Rusty and spend some time with my furry friends. On the drive home my friend and I excitedly told him all about our experiences in class and what we were going to do with it, how it would fit into our lives and how we couldn't wait to get started.

I walked into my front door full of excitement about starting up my angel work and doing past life healings. I put my suitcases down, walked to my kitchen and checked my phone messages. My life was about to change. The first message was from the vet telling me that she didn't like leaving the sort of message on a phone that she was about to leave. She said there was no indication that what happened was going to happen. Everything had seemed OK when they had gone home in the evening, but when they got there in the morning Rusty has passed away sometime in the night and I should call them before I went to the clinic. My heart stopped. What went through my mind was – Angels! How could you do this to me? I was prepared to go all out and start my work. What is going on? I was beside myself. My mind was in turmoil. This couldn't be right!

The next message was from one of the pet rescuers telling me I would have a strange message on my phone that Rusty had died but that he really hadn't. I was to call her as soon as I got in as he wasn't in good shape and a decision had to be made, but she felt it was my decision to make. I was more confused than ever. The next message was from my daughter telling me the same thing and insisting I call her right away.

I called the pet rescuer back but she wasn't home. The next call I made was to the vet clinic. I spoke with the vet who was obviously distraught. She said there was no indication of how badly off Rusty was. He had the run of the clinic and seemed to be doing OK. He was found in his kennel that morning with no

> **Blessings**
>
> *Your angels and loved ones in spirit are showering you with blessings.*
>
> *Though you may have experienced recent challenges, you are truly loved and blessed by those who constantly watch over you. They have never left your side. Open yourself up to receive their comfort and blessings.*

heartbeat and was cold to the touch. She said a short time later he was alive but they had no idea how this could be. The kennel cleaner looked over and noticed his tail twitch so they started him on an intravenous drip immediately. I was having trouble keeping up and understanding what exactly was going on. She said I would have to come down to the clinic and do an assessment and decide on next steps. She told me he had brain damage. At that point I already knew what the decision needed to be, but they wanted me at the clinic. I called my daughter to tell her I was on my way to the clinic. She offered to go with me but I wanted to handle this myself.

I only live a few minutes from the clinic but the drive felt very long. I went into the kennel room and saw Rusty through the bars. His pupils were vertical slits and I knew his brain damage was too extensive. I called his name and took him into my arms. He responded to my voice so I knew he recognized me. My boy had come back to life so we could say goodbye. I spent the next couple of hours in the vet's office holding Rusty and telling him how much I loved him. I told him I would miss him but he needed to go home with the angels. I told the clinic staff I was going to release him from his pain and each of them came in to say goodbye. The vet came in with syringe in hand, kissed Rusty on the head, talked to me for awhile and said "Mom, this is it," and inserted the fluid into his intravenous. Rusty left this world peacefully while cradled in my arms. I gently laid him down, covered him with a blanket and said a final goodbye.

Everything I learned and everything I had planned from angel class had left my head. I couldn't focus on any of the angel stuff. My heart was broken and I felt I had failed a dear friend. The healing was a slow process. I took his picture and put angel wings on it and a halo. His picture became my desktop background so I could see him every day. What was it with this tabby cat that had such an impact on me? I had lost other pets.

The evolution was slow but his photo with wings and halo became my logo. My business became a reality and the name represented Rusty: 'Wings of Healing.' The Past Life Regression workshop with my two friends finally manifested in April 2010. I plan on creating a deck of angel cards with the cats I have fostered being paired with angels and goddesses. My animal communication and healing CD is dedicated to Rusty. During the creation of the last meditation, which is about communicating with your deceased pet, Rusty came to me and told me he was the keeper of the gate. He will be the one to meet you at the gate of heaven, walk you through the gate, and guide you to your deceased pet for a visitation.

Rusty was with me for six short months but in those months he gave me a lifetime worth of love. He showed me my path of working with animals for healing and communication. It took several months for me to work through my grief for this wonderful, loving soul, but he is with me now every step of the way as I move forward in my angel work. He not only showed me that anything is possible when one loves enough, but that communication and healing work both ways.

Connecting with a Deceased Pet with Archangel Sandalphon

There is a special place, deep within where the gifts of healing, love and inner strength await you. That place is calling to you now, asking you to slow down, set the world aside and give yourself this gift of peace and relaxation. To prepare for this journey to meet and speak with your deceased pet, make sure you won't be disturbed for about 15 minutes. Relax your body by breathing in for the count of 7, hold for 7, and breathe out for 7. Repeat this several times. Breathe in relaxation and love; breathe out stress and tension. Breathe in peace and tranquility, breathe out anger and fear. Feel your body relax, starting at your toes, your legs, your abdomen. All tension in your muscles relaxes now. Your muscles feel like limp, loose rope. Continue to breathe deeply and slowly, relaxing deeper and deeper.

You find yourself at the base of a staircase that winds up into the heavens. The air around you is quiet and still. The lighting is a soft blue as it wraps itself around you. You start your ascent up the stairs. As you come to a bend in the staircase you see Archangel Sandalphon standing there. He has come to join you on your visit to your deceased pet. He tells you "Dear one, I am here to comfort and guide you on your journey." You continue up the stairs with Archangel Sandalphon by your side. As you move up the stairs you begin to hear angelic music. It wafts down the staircase and dispels any further tension you may have on this journey with its beautiful melody. You continue upwards towards the music. Soon you can see a glistening gate of gold ahead of you. When you reach the gate, Rusty, a handsome male tabby cat with beautiful golden eyes, is there to greet you. He tells you he is the gate keeper and will guide your way to your destination and assist you in any way in communicating with your beloved animal. The gates open and Rusty leads you and Archangel Sandalphon down a winding path of golden cobblestones.

You come to an open field bathed with a soft, misty gold light. As you peer through the mist, you see your deceased animal relaxing in the middle of the field. They greet you warmly and you give them a hug. The first thing they tell you is that they still feel connected to you and your family. Ask them for an example of what that means. Be still and listen to what they have to tell you.

Relaxed by this, you ask if they are happy. You ask if they are going to come back to you in your lifetime. If the answer is yes, ask them how, in what body, when? Trust that what you receive is the truth. Take a few moments to tell them how much you miss them, but understand they are happy and well where they are now. Take a few moments and tell them anything else you want them to know. Ask them any more questions you would like answers to. Ask Archangel Sandalphon and Rusty to assist you if you are confused by what you hear, or need clarification. They are there to provide you with love and support.

When you have finished your conversation, thank your pet, give them another hug and tell them you will come back and talk to them again soon. Feeling at peace and loved, you let Archangel Sandalphon take your hand to start the way back to the present time. Rusty turns and leads the way back down the winding path of gold. When you reach the gates of gold that are the exit, Rusty bids you farewell and says, "I will be here at the gate until your return, making sure all is safe." You thank him, and you and Archangel Sandalphon descend the staircase.

At the bottom of the stairs, Archangel Sandalphon gives you one final message from your animal and a gift with which to remember this time you had together. He then hugs you and says, "I will be waiting for you when you decide to return to visit your deceased friend again."

When you are ready, gently and slowly come back to this time.

This is a meditation from my *Healing for You & Your Pets* CD, dedicated to Rusty, who lived and died so I might learn.

Music

*Your angels wish to uplift your spirits
through music and song.*

*Singing or listening to gentle music
will revive your spirits, and provide a
welcome respite from your daily cares.
The soothing power of music to relax
your mind and calm your soul allows
you to be more open to receiving
heaven-sent gifts.*

DENICE MARTIN
Mornington Peninsula, Victoria, Australia

DENICE MARTIN is a gifted medium and intuitive clairvoyant healer who works with the angelic and spiritual realm. She has studied at a number of Universities in the field of education, obtaining a Graduate Certificate in Fraud Investigation at La Trobe University in Melbourne, having worked in this field since 1997.

She began her own business in the spiritual realm in early 2007 and teaches meditation and psychic awareness classes when not seeing clients or writing. She travels frequently to explore the world. Denice's gifts have been with her from early childhood. As a youngster she only spoke of them with her paternal grandmother from whom she had inherited them. It was after her grandmother passed on that her true gifts blossomed. She has three grown children of which two are also gifted in this same way and a granddaughter who has already displayed obvious signs of spiritual conversations.

Denice is a writer and poet who is currently developing a number of works for publication in the near future. She is an inspiring person who leads others with direction and confidence and states that this is more fulfilling than anything else she could achieve on her own. Denice attributes her successes to those from the Angelic realm who channel their guidance and wisdom directly through her and onto the pages as she writes.

If you would like to experience a private consultation or register for one of her classes, please visit Denice at: www.rainbowangel.vpweb.com.au

Believe

DENICE MARTIN

The proof that we continue living without a physical body
comes through clearly whenever I see clients for a reading or healing.

On the Pacific Ocean, the weather was humid and steamy. I was on holiday with a group of friends on a cruise ship. After much sunshine I decided to retreat to a quiet area of the ship. I found a lounge chair and lay down for some peace and much-needed rest. One of our friends joined me, and as we sat chatting and relaxing, I began to tell her of my visions and clairvoyance. She said that I should develop myself further and attend a spiritual circle. I found this daunting as I had not spoken to anyone about my gift before. I was given the name of an elderly lady who ran a circle in Melbourne, so, at the end of the cruise, I phoned her to explain what had been happening with me. I was pleasantly surprised when she asked me to join her group.

This wonderful lady taught me all aspects of Mediumship and the importance of managing it correctly. I'd had this gift from childhood and had learnt to live with it but didn't really think of it as anything special. I had always seen spirit and had only recently begun seeing angels. I believe this was happening because my vibration level had changed and I had moved to a higher level of awareness.

What I wanted most though, was to meet with my own personal guardian angel. So with that intention I made it my focus when I meditated to do just that. Since I meditate every day, I was becoming quite frustrated that I had only received messages and saw no visible sight of my personal guardian angel. One day I went into a deep meditation with this full intention. I found myself gliding up a steep hill and all the while had a strong feeling that this journey was going to be worth the experience. The closer I moved to the top of the hill, the greener the grass became. More and more flowers surrounded me and the fragrance was spectacular, something I have never had the privilege of smelling before in my entire life. The sun was beaming and I could feel its warmth on my face and skin. I felt as if it were the first day of summer after a lingering winter. I raised my face to the sky to enjoy it more and as looked up, I saw only the bluest and clearest of color.

In the distance I could see what appeared to be a building. As I drew closer, it became clearer to me that it was a building with no roof and large pillars dividing each quadrant or sector. This building was surrounded by trees which lined the boundary, connected to a pair of huge iron gates in the shape of wings. There was no one else around that I could see but I sensed that there were many others there. My hands reached for the gates wondering how I could open them when suddenly and quietly they began to slowly open. The minute they opened I suddenly heard angelic music playing, something I could not hear earlier when the gates were closed. The voices I heard were so soft and clear! I noticed how serene it was here and immediately relaxed. It was as if a weight had been lifted from my shoulders and I had not a care in the world.

A soft light appeared in the distance and as I moved closer, I could see what appeared to be a small female child. I knew I was heading in the right direction. The child was wearing a long white gown and looked similar to me when I was much younger. My heart filled with the deepest feelings. As she took my hand, I had tears in my eyes and my heart swelled inside my chest. I have never before felt such a bond. It was the most truly amazing feeling. We walked together not uttering a word. It was as if we were floating not walking towards a light. I observed everything around me and saw that the colors were more vivid and brilliant than ever. The setting was very tranquil. I noticed a waterfall in the distance to the right of the light. The waterfall had a lovely grassed area and a body of water at its base like a large lake. There were flowers in small circles everywhere and their colors were crystal clear and very bright. In front of us was a two seated chair made from tree branches, the seats covered in fresh leaves. The child motioned for me to sit here so I could contemplate what was happening.

The young child moved a few feet away, towards the watery edge. She held her hand up for me to stay seated which I did. She seemed to be staring out into the direction of the middle of the lake. I watched her intently as she stepped onto the water. It was as if the water had a glass surface. Even though I couldn't see her feet, I knew she was gliding toward the center. As I observed this child, I saw what appeared to be a very bright white light shining onto the water in the center of the lake. This beam of light became brighter and brighter and the child stopped midway. Then as I watched this light, I saw what appeared to be the shape of a lady in a long white gown. The light still surrounded her and seemed to expand, making her more visible to me. As the light expanded I could clearly see that she had wings which unfolded from around her. They were a clear translucent white and were extremely large, larger than I could ever have imagined. I stood in awe of this beautiful sight.

The young child was standing close by this beautiful angel and beckoned for me to move closer to the watery edge. As I stood at the edge of the lake, I became enveloped in enormous warmth which completely surrounded my entire body. I felt the greatest surge of love, more than I have ever experienced in my life. This lovely angel put her hands out as if to call me closer. The angel and child both began moving closer, floating towards me. This was the most beautiful sight I have ever seen. I felt the most amazing sensation entering my body. The angel approached me on the grassy area and held my hand. We moved back to the chair and the child sat at our feet. As I faced the angel, I noticed the angel's eyes were very large and oval shaped. Her lips never moved but I could hear her words clearly. As I listened, I understood each and every word she spoke. At last I completely understood what my life path was to be. Through this type of telepathy, she told me I had healing qualities and that I would indeed be sought after in respect to communication with the angels and spirit through Mediumship.

Even though my abilities were strong, and although I had intended on many occasions to meet with my spirit guide or guardian angel, prior to this I had not been successful. However after this first meeting, I realized that the timing must not have been right before.

This wonderful being is my guardian angel and her name is Mariel. Whenever I do readings, healings or teach, I feel her presence immediately when I ask to connect with her. She fills my very soul with the same warmth as she did on that first day. I feel my vibration changing to a much higher level than ever before. This beautiful angel speaks to me clearly and always assists me when I am communicating with spirit. The messages brought through are filled with comfort and love from those who have departed from this physical world. The proof that we continue living without a physical body comes through clearly whenever I see clients for a reading or healing. I always ask my client not to disclose anything and if the information I am giving them is relevant, to only acknowledge this with a simple yes or no.

Communicating with my angel also helps in other situations. I can always ask Mariel for guidance or assistance at any time. You see I have three children. The youngest is clairaudient and my eldest is clairvoyant like me. *Clair* is the French word for clear and *audient* is for hearing, while *voyant* is for sight or seeing. My youngest daughter meditates frequently and receives messages so I continue to teach her how to refine this technique.

On a particular night she was awoken by a strong negative energy. This male energy was quite aggressive in his language and this frightened her to the point where she was literally quite scared and started crying. My daughter is twenty-two and doesn't take any type of illicit drugs nor had she had any type of alcohol that night. She was so frightened that she called me to see if I could help her.

I had been successful in calming her down and asked her to go into meditation. I instructed her to ask her guidance to dissipate this energy and to surround her with protection in the form of a brilliant bubble of white light so this and any other negative energy could not return. Whilst she was doing this, I went into meditation myself and asked for Mariel and all of my angels and guides to work with my daughter's guides and angels to remove this energy and prevent it from returning. They did so, and we both felt a very powerful healing energy going to work. Once this work was completed, she returned to sleep.

I also went back to sleep only to be woken by the energy that had been bothering my daughter. I don't know how I knew it was the same, but I did. I could clearly see this male energy standing at the foot of my bed. I bolted upright and as I sat there, in my mind I called for Mariel. This energy was standing with his arms crossed in front of him and was very angry. He had such a defiant stance and a sly look on his face. I made sure he knew that he was never to return his presence to my daughter and that he would be dealing with me. I actually meant that statement in the way a mother would, by protecting her child against harm and not from any angelic or spiritual point of view.

Within what appeared to be seconds, a group of six angels were surrounding him. One was Mariel, and as their powerful energy seemed to touch each other I could see it expand around the room. It was so brilliant. The negative energy was dispersed.

My daughter now has two protective guardian energies which remind her of wolves, who surround and protect her constantly. She feels she has a calmness surrounding her soul whenever she has a heightened vibration now. When she awoke after that particular night, she felt she had never slept so well. She remembers this incident and is still affected by it to this day. But she always remembers the importance of surrounding herself with the purest of white light and calling on her own angels for protection if she ever requires help.

In the eighties I had an extraordinary angel experience which involved my middle daughter who at that time was only six months of age. She contracted a terrible virus which the medical experts suspected was Meningitis. I rushed her to the emergency room at our local country hospital. I was hysterical and prayed hard for assistance from God or the Angels to bring her back from the brink of death. I struggled with my own rational mind but overrode it and kept my belief in my Guardian Angels. I knew they could help either to heal my baby or gather her in their arms and take her home so she wouldn't be afraid.

I was concentrating so much on my daughter that I didn't really notice that no one else acknowledged the person standing in front of me, apart from myself. I soon realized that this person was actually an Angel, and with all my heart I thanked her. She placed one hand on my baby and one on me. I then felt the strongest surge of love. I held my daughter's tiny limp body in my arms and kissed her forehead. As I held my beautiful baby in my arms, another energy entered the room. My

---

Guardian Angel

Your Guardian Angel loves you very much.

You are not alone. Your Angel has always been with you to love and support you on your journey through this lifetime. Your Guardian Angel loves you unconditionally and will never leave your side.

daughter was rushed to a larger hospital which had a Pediatric wing. Numerous tests were completed and after three days I was able to take her back home. Today she is twenty five and I cannot tell you how many times I have thanked the Angels for their help at that time.

When I talk of the messages that are given to me during a reading I have to admit that they are sometimes heard very clearly, as whispers. Pictures or words are just impressed on my mind. The impressions however, are extremely clear and very precise and I must add, always in color. I have always dreamt in color as well, and thought this was normal for everyone. I have always remembered my dreams and now believe that most are not only recollections of past lives I have lived, but also visitations from my angels and spirit friends, giving messages of love and support and future information that I need.

Recently while sleeping, I had obviously begun astral traveling when I met Mariel who took me to a place which seemed quite three dimensional. I knew from this that what I was seeing and feeling was another plane of existence. Whether it was the spirit world or the afterlife, I am still unsure. But while I was there I was shown some specific symbols which lay in a circular pattern on a grassy field. These symbols were to have significance for me at a later time. This information was relayed to me from two Archangels, Raphael and Gabriel.

When the two Archangels appeared I was in awe of their beauty and the love which exuded from them. As they moved closer to me, I felt my whole vibration change and rise to an entirely new level. To give you an idea of what I felt, can you remember as a child holding two magnets together and the force that you felt as they pushed against each other? This is what I feel when any angelic force moves close to my aura and surrounds me with such warmth.

I awoke very excited by the dream and fortunately, having my notebook with me, I drew the symbols as they had appeared to me, along with the diagrams of the pattern and how it lay. I also sketched the Archangels. My talents certainly do not lie in the field of art but I drew them just as I saw them. To me, they are the most beautiful angelic beings I have ever witnessed.

Not long ago, I had a call from a young man and detected urgency in his voice. He requested a one hour appointment as soon as possible. On the day he was to visit me, I had meditated as I usually do and Mariel came to me and showed me clearly what was troubling this young man. Usually when my clients arrive, I offer them refreshment and ask them not to disclose anything to me prior to the reading. We make general chit chat until the reading begins so that the vibration in my clients' voices can initiate the angelic and spiritual contact.

Once the reading began I was looking at my client when I saw a shape appearing behind him. My client was quite nervous and as I reassured him that everything would be OK, this shape behind him became clearer, revealing that it was that of a Maori person. I knew from this that my client was of Maori origin and told him of the name which was given to me. You would never have guessed he was from

New Zealand as he had a definite Australian accent. My client was so shocked that he almost choked on his glass of water. He said that no-one would know that person as he was adopted from birth and that the name that I gave him was that of his birth father. My client had only learned this himself a short time previous to our meeting as he had been searching for his real birth family. He had suffered a lot of anxiety during his young life and was still greatly troubled.

As the reading progressed, the Maori figure stepped back and stood next to a shadow which had also appeared earlier. I could clearly see the outline of this shadow, and as my client spoke, the shadow began to transform into an angel. The angel moved closer toward him and placed her hands gently on his shoulders. At the very moment this took place, my client placed his right hand on his left shoulder. When I asked him why, he said he could feel warmth in that area. As my client had acknowledged the feeling, the figure became excited that she was being acknowledged. I asked my client to close his eyes and as he did she unfolded her wings and wrapped them around his whole body. My client could feel this intense warmth and described it as the most unbelievable feeling he had ever felt.

My client was receiving a powerful healing and as I witnessed this event even I was a little taken aback. I could clearly see a colorful cloud of what appeared to be a mist swirling around my client. It moved very gently from this beautiful angel's heart and entered my client directly through his heart chakra. The colors were so soft, similar to the colors of the rainbow. This lasted around three minutes and when the angel had finished, she placed her hand on his heart and then disappeared. My client opened his eyes and said that whatever I had done that I should bottle it, as he had never felt more relaxed and at peace. I described my vision and asked him what he had experienced. He said it was as if he were wrapped in an electric blanket and that he had an incredibly warm sensation traveling through his entire body. He felt calm and for the first time in his life, instead of feeling anxious, he now felt full of love.

As I explained the appearance of the Maori figure and the angel, I told my client that the Maori figure was in fact his birth father's father and that he would lead him to his birth family in New Zealand. My client was astonished as he had previously booked a flight back to New Zealand and was scheduled to leave in three weeks. I mentioned the name of the town where he needed to go and he asked if I was sure. I said no, I wasn't sure, but this was the message that had been passed on by both presences during the reading. He was encouraged to continue on his search to see what he could find out. After a couple of months this client sent me an email and stated that not only had he found his birth family, but he had found them in the town I had mentioned in the reading. He was very grateful to me, but I told him it wasn't me he had to be grateful to, but his angels. For it was his own angel giving such clarity and good expert guidance!

Believing in my gift, a tiny seed which grew, saw me helping others as only time could tell; for what I say is true now: believe and you will too, for we all have the power and know just what to do. Wrap them in pure love, blocking out all fear, asking just for guidance; believe and you will hear.

An Angel Influenced Meditation
This is a guided meditation to help you to feel centered, supported and self-loved.

First imagine yourself walking high on a grassy mountain slope amidst the warmth of a summer day. As you reach the peak of the mountain, sit gently on the warm grass. As you do, raise your face in the direction of the sky and feel the warm sun on your cheeks. You notice that the sky is free from any clouds except one small white fluffy one, which appears to be moving slowly towards you.

As this cloud comes closer, you see that it is a very small cloud, but large enough to carry two people. It hovers alongside you but doesn't touch the ground. Now an angel appears, standing on the cloud and she beckons for you to climb on. You take her hand gently and rest next to her as the cloud starts to move away from the mountain.

Not a word is spoken between you and your angel, but you know that this is where you are meant to be and feel perfectly safe and calm. You soon notice a tiny island, and the cloud moves closer to the sand where you and the angel alight. You both begin to walk on the sand which feels warm under your feet. You have so much clarity that you can even identify the tiny grains of sand which are caught between your toes. You see a hammock resting between two palm trees and your angel gestures for you to lie down on it and close your eyes. You are aware of the soothing sound of waves gently lapping the sand, and you listen to their constant swoosh as they ebb and flow.

You know your angel is still present but you now also feel the presence of other angels. As you open your eyes, you see that you are surrounded by a large group of angels exuding love, beauty and warmth. Your angel asks you to release all that troubles you. As you look around, you see that all the angels have both hands, palms up directed at you to accept your troubles and remove them from your mind. You then close your eyes again and release everything that you feel is negative or weighing on your mind. As you do this, you feel lightened, as though a very heavy weight has been removed. When you open your eyes, the group of angels has disappeared and they've taken all your troubles with them.

Your angel beckons for you to follow her now. As you move along the sand, you come to a shaded area, surrounded by rocks and a waterfall. This body of water is flowing gently, and you listen to the gentle sounds of splashing as the water falls into the lake. Your angel asks you to move and stand under the waterfall to cleanse and purify your body. You do so and are amazed that the water is warm.

Not only does the water feel warm but you feel it running through your veins and into your heart. Your body now exudes pure love, and you feel at one with yourself and nature. You understand that you have now been cleansed and that all negative energies have been replaced with positive, happy thoughts and feelings. You look toward your angel who is standing by the lake. You move toward her and look at both reflections in the water. You are both surrounded by a beautiful translucent golden light which glows brilliantly and beams directly up into the sky. You feel centered and whole.

The little cloud appears to take you back to your original place of rest. You feel as if you have been transported to another place and time where nothing matters except Divine Love. You thank your angel and head back down the mountain to your Home, feeling as though your journey has not come to an end but has only just begun.

You open your eyes to feel refreshed, loved and supported. You begin to understand what is important in your life and what you can hold onto and what you must release to be more fulfilled in your life. You know now that your contribution to any of your relationships will be more positive, understanding and full of compassion, as you feel the magnitude of the events which have come from your journey with your angel.

Pure guidance and Divine Love has touched your soul today. It's a good idea to write a journal that will capture all of your meditation experiences. You can view these at a time when you feel you need reassurance and support. Every time you read of your angelic experiences, you invoke the presence of your angel, and she will be with you to support and nourish your soul.

◯

Intuition

Your angels are whispering to you now through your natural intuition.

Though you may dismiss them at first, the messages you are receiving through your dreams, visions, feelings, your inner voice or a deep sense of knowing are very real. It is safe to trust your own intuition and pay attention to this heavenly guidance.

DE-ARNE KING
Sydney, Australia

DE-ARNE has been aware of her intuition from a very early age. Being a sensitive little girl she could feel energies, see, and hear things that others couldn't. This frightened her until she was much older. Study with several sages helped her to understand and trust in her inner knowing.

She represented her region in national hairdressing championships, excelling in advanced hairdressing education before embracing her analytical left brain in the corporate arena prior to starting a business as a consultant bookkeeper until affectionately being "nudged" back into her right brain and into the angelic realms she now embraces.

De-Arne is an Angel Intuitive™ certified by Doreen Virtue Ph.D. She works closely with the angelic realms, archangels and ascended masters, who give their help and guidance through her healing modalities. As an Angel Intuitive™, she incorporates angel readings and healings into her practice. De-Arne is also a certified Reiki Practitioner, ThetaHealing™ Practitioner, Clairvoyant Healing Practitioner and Animal Communicator. As an Animal Communicator De-Arne incorporates working with missing animals and animals that have passed. Crystals are a passion and she embraces their healing energies in her practice. She also studied Bach Flower Remedies, Aromatherapy and Astrology. De-Arne continues studying various complementary metaphysics including Mediumship and is also currently studying as a trainee teacher in the techniques of The Billings Ovulation Method™ of Natural Fertility Awareness. Born in New Zealand, De-Arne now makes her home in Sydney, Australia with her husband.

You can email De-Arne at angel.whispers@live.com.au

Angels In My Mist

DE-ARNE KING

The great pleasure and feeling in my right brain
is more than my left brain can find the words to tell you.

—NOBEL LAUREATE ROGER SPERRY

One of my earliest memories is of me around the age of three talking to my grandmother who looked after me whilst my mother worked. I was very loved by my grandmother who knitted cardigans and sweaters and sewed beautiful dresses for me. When she died, my family was very sad and we missed her very much. My mother recalls being woken in the night hearing me giggling and talking. When she asked me who I was talking to, I told her I was talking to nana who had smiled at me and was talking to me, and that I wanted to be with my nana. When she told me nana had died and gone to heaven, we affectionately gave her the name of Nana-in-Heaven. This early childhood memory was the start of my journey communicating with my spirit guides, angels and the Creator.

I remember many times throughout my childhood when I had what I considered 'eerie' experiences, mostly during the night – waking to see outlines of people standing beside my bed, having my feet tickled or experiencing strange dreams. Of course, I didn't know what was happening but I remember being terrified and sometimes hopping into bed with my parents, being too scared to stay in my own bed. Sadly, it was not until much later that I realized one of my visitors who tickled my feet was my Nana-in-Heaven and another visitor was my great grandfather who I was also very close to. In hindsight, it was obvious it was him as he remained dressed in his signature 'going out' suit and hat. They have both remained with me all my life and are two of my spirit guides.

As a teenager, my intuition started to flow through prophetic dreams being shared with me by the angels. These dreams were in color, with great detail and sound. My understanding is that these angel messages came to me in dream form, as I was a little scared when they appeared in any other format, like visitations during the night. As a teenager, I did not understand yet that the angels are God's messengers and are here to help us for our best and highest good.

One dream the angels shared with me was of one of my schoolteacher's being pregnant. I remember feeling that this was quite cool; I had insider knowledge. Being a young teenager, I recall blurting out in class, "Miss, I had a dream last night that you are pregnant." I clearly recall her saying "And you Miss, are on detention." Hmmm, that threw me. A short time later in another dream, the angels shared with me again, that my teacher was pregnant and would be going away on maternity leave and the next time I would see her, she would be walking towards me pushing her baby boy in a stroller along the school hallway. Having learnt from my first outburst, I showed some discernment and this time waited until all the students had left the classroom. I stayed behind and said to my teacher "You can put me on detention if you want but I have been shown another dream that you are pregnant and you are having a boy." I was pleasantly surprised, as this time my teacher said to me "If you promise not to tell anyone, I am pregnant." I guess this was my first real validation that what the angels were sharing with me was true. And yes, the next time I saw the teacher when she returned to the school, she was walking down the school corridor towards me pushing her baby boy in his stroller.

Having these types of dreams was quite routine for me and I often found myself waking with 'inside knowledge' from the angels and waiting for this knowledge to become 'general knowledge' in what we now term the 'muggle' world, thanks to J. K. Rowling and the *Harry Potter* books. More often than not, the dreams would be of pregnancies, births and loved ones who had passed over.

I have the occasional nightmare and when I do, I quickly call on Archangel Michael to be by my side and protect me. I have witnessed him fill my bedroom with indigo blue and white sparkles, instantly helping me to feel calm in the knowledge that he is there with me.

The Angelic Realm, although never far from my thoughts, was not always as openly accepted in my general day-to-day existence. I learnt to keep the angelic communications to myself whilst learning and soaking up anything and every-thing about spirituality that I could. It has not been uncommon for some people throughout my life to think I am a little 'out there.' I have always been known to say, "Let me ask my faeries" or "My angels told me." It has always been a blessing to know that I had the support of these beautiful ones who were only a moment's thought away, ready and waiting to help guide me when I requested their help.

Whilst still a teenager, my mother and I connected with a spiritual circle (a group of people who meet to discuss like-minded interests). We gathered to medi-tate and pray, sending loving and healing energies out to the rest of the world. I was too young to value exactly what I was involved in at the time, but looking back, I have a clearer understanding of how calling on the angels for their help really does work universally. By using the power of thought and sending out healing energies to others, we were sharing divine, angelic, energetic love to help heal the universe.

It was not until very much later in my life that I embraced the Angelic Realm

again. After finding myself waking up in the recovery room after a surgical procedure, very ill, and hearing nurses whispering "She stopped breathing after surgery,"
my life direction significantly changed, even if I didn't realize this at first. I spent
many months recovering and with a lot of time on my hands, I found myself reas-
sessing my life. I had a very real urge to re-embrace my soul's journey.

One day while buying crystals in my local spiritual shop, I met an intuitive
woman and even though I had not had a 'reading' for years, I felt drawn to her
serene energy. I found myself sitting with her in her room as she read some of
Doreen Virtue's *Angel Cards*, amongst the other modalities she offered. I remember
leaving the reading with a knowing that angels and the Creator were surrounding
me and I was clearer in my direction ahead. I did not fully understand at the time
what she meant when she told me that all I needed was within me, that the angels
were always eager to help me, and that all I needed to do was to call them to my
side. This reading started me on my journey of awareness in what I have coined
my 'University of Intuition,' an ongoing learning about the *Clairs – clairvoyance*
(seeing), *clairsentinence* (sensing), *clairsentience* (feeling), *claircognizance* (knowing),
clairaudience (hearing), *clairalience* (smelling) and *clairgustance* (tasting).

As I set off on this journey, the angels began introducing me to many beautiful
Earth Angels. I have learnt how to turn my gifts on and off, and how to share the
angels' words with others through angel readings and healings. There have been
many times when both my client and I have been bowled over by the information
or healings that are shared with us via the angels. One of my first angel healings
was for a client who had had a knee injury for many years from playing tennis. He
had been wearing two knee guards on the one knee for 2 or 3 years. This injury
at times prevented him from being able to bend his knee or walk properly and it
caused intense pain. He was very skeptical and didn't believe in healings and such
things, but his wife suggested that he try it anyway. The pain was very intense
and at this point my client knew that having a healing wasn't going to make the
knee any worse.

I prepared myself for the healing and called in my favorite angels to request
healing for my client: Archangel Michael, whose healing color is blue and whose
name means 'He who is like God,' and Archangel Raphael, whose soothing color
is emerald green and whose name means 'God heals.' Among the many things
Archangel Michael helps with is releasing fear, and Archangel Raphael assists with
healings. These two have never let me down and this healing was extra special
because my client, who had been skeptical, experienced an instant healing and
became pain free. This healing was several years ago now and he still remains
pain free. This former skeptic has even spoken about his healing to others including his General Practitioner. He has experienced some skepticism whilst sharing
his healing experience but despite this he remains a believer. This same client has
since received relief for an arm injury via distance healing and the reiki angels,
thus supporting his confidence in energetic healing.

Having a belief and good intent for the best and highest good of the client is all that is needed to heal with the angels. We all have angels we can call upon, and they are very happy to share their guidance and healing with us. It is uncomplicated. All you need to do is ask and it shall be done – as long as it is within the realms of love, and being for the best and highest good of all concerned. The angels will never intervene in our free will unless we are in a life-threatening situation. They are omnipresent and can be in many places all at the same time. So do not feel you are interrupting them when you call on them for help. They are waiting eagerly to help us with anything and everything, from finding lost objects, car parking spaces, mental clarity for study and recall of information, to energetic healing.

My introduction to meeting my guardian angel was an awesome experience. I was in a group being visually guided through meditation, having grounded ourselves and opening our chakras, we were to meet and introduce ourselves to our guardian angel. I find myself relaxing quickly when meditating within group energy and I recall seeing my guardian angel quite quickly, but was thrown a little as I saw two males present themselves. I could clearly see the detail of the guardian angel I didn't know, dressed in long flowing robes. He held a staff in his hand, had longish hair, and his energy was of pure love and protection. The other male I recognized as my great grandfather who is always with me and one of my spirit guides. We were guided to ask our guardian angel's name and I remember feeling quite disappointed when I could not get a name from my guardian angel. This left me feeling confused as my classmates all seemed to have their guardian angels' names and were excitedly chatting to each other about them.

We broke for a bathroom break and I remember asking for the name to be shared with me. My head felt like it was going to explode because I was trying so hard to hear or see the name. As I came out of the cubicle I remember cracking up laughing as my guardian angel's name boomed into my head, loud and clear. I am not sure if it was the loud voice or the surrounds that made me laugh but I felt like I had just met my new best friend! My spirit guide and guardian angel had had a bit of a standoff as both wanted to be my protector. They came to an understanding and I now have both looking out for me. Whenever I need help or guidance my guardian angel is the first angel I call upon.

I recently received an SOS text message from a friend asking for angelic help by way of giving her 11 year old daughter a distant healing as she was in hospital with meningitis.

Meningitis is an inflammation of the protective membranes covering the spinal cord and brain. The child's body was covered in a rash and she was awaiting a lumbar puncture to confirm exactly what type she had, either viral or bacterial. A lumbar puncture is a needle placed into the spine to remove spinal fluid for testing. My friend's daughter was terrified. She said she felt like she was fading and terrified she was going to die. I remember praying to Archangel Michael, Archangel Raphael, Mother Mary and the Creator to be with the young girl to calm her, heal her and to give her a speedy recovery. I could see the angels surrounding the young girl's hospital bed. The room was glowing with light as they were giving her a healing and I knew that all would be well. After I returned a text message explaining what I had witnessed, I immediately received a call from my friend who excitedly relayed what her daughter had just shared with her.

Her daughter had been asleep and when she awoke, she told her mother she knew that the angels were with her, and that she was surrounded by light. She could see the angels by her side and she felt she was floating out of her body as the angels lifted her and were helping her to get well. My friend was so amazed that her daughter had relayed everything I had texted to her. She is a very intuitive young girl and very in tune with her angels. There was much relief in the family when their daughter was discharged from hospital the following day. Her rash had disappeared overnight, and she quickly recovered in the comfort of her home.

This same young girl helped me on the morning of a procedure I had scheduled. I was particularly nervous after my previous experience with surgery. Being better prepared, I had called in the Archangels Michael and Raphael and felt their presence with me, but I texted my girlfriend for emotional support anyway. Since she was driving her daughter to school, her daughter read the text out loud to her mother. She went on to declare that I would be okay because she knew the angels were with me, because she could see Archangel Michael by my side. I recall waking up from surgery and being surrounding in a mist of blue. I knew at that point just how protected I was by that angel mist; Archangel Michael had his wings wrapped around me. The surgery went extremely well with no adverse reactions this time.

Meditation

You will hear your angels more clearly the more your mind is relaxed.

Practice quieting your mind by closing your eyes, breathing deeply and allowing yourself to relax. The answers you seek from your angels will come to you more clearly when you take time out each day to meditate.

Automatic writing is another way of communing with the angels, guides and the Creator. I particularly love this form of communication and find the angels sharing information with me as I type on my computer. I prefer to type as I can get more words down than handwriting them, because the angels talk so quickly. They can be quite funny, on one occasion coming through in French until I asked them to speak in English. However, the French words that were shared with my client were relevant, personal and were understood, even as I wrote some of them phonetically – I don't speak French. I am continually amazed with the accuracy of their messages and blessed to be able to share them and bring a sense of peace and understanding to the recipient of the message.

As I continued along my journey, I was reading everything I could get my hands on. It is common for me to have numerous books on my bedside table, all being read in some capacity. Some are reference material and others are read by osmosis, by just being beside my bed. It still amazes me when I pick up a book from my bedside table and start reading, only to find the information is familiar and leaves me wondering if I have in fact already read that book. Doreen Virtue's book the *Lightworker's Way* was probably the first of her books that I read, and from that moment, I had a yearning to learn as much as I could about the angels. Then in 2009, when a girlfriend suggested we attend the Doreen Virtue Angel Intuitive Course in the beautiful lush surrounds of the Sunshine Coast in Queensland, Australia, I was excited!

The day we arrived, I took photographs of the resort. We were staying at the beautiful Hyatt Regency Coolum, which is set amongst a tropical background of lush green palms, exotic-scented flowering plants and an excellent championship golf course. The vegetation seemed huge and we were entertained to see brush turkeys strolling around the gardens, fossicking for food and sneaking leftover cappuccino's left on the tables. It was around three in the afternoon on one of those glorious sunny and cloud-free spring days in November with the temperature around 28 degrees Celsius and we were feeling the energy of the location. I am an avid photographer and starting taking photos of the gardens surrounding our room. But the images in every photo I took were shrouded in cloud-like mist. This excited us because we knew that the area was blanketed in 'angel mist' and that we were in for an awesome weekend with like-minded Angel Lightworkers, under the guidance of Doreen and the angels.

Throughout the weekend we learnt many techniques to connect with the angels. One of my favorites was a meditation where Doreen guided us to meet some of the angels she named individually, sharing a little of what each angel is here to help us with. We also learnt about the differing Angelic Realms and were delighted when an Incarnated Elemental, a leprechaun dressed up in human clothing, entertained us. He was everything we perceived a leprechaun to be. He was mischievous and funny, playing pranks on the Earth Angels and generally making people laugh and feel good. It was enlightening to learn what realm we belonged to, and to be introduced to the ever-evolving new realms. The last morning before we left for the airport, I took photos again of the garden area surrounding our room. This time the digital photographs were bright and clear; the angel mist had lifted.

I often take photos of the faeries and angels by pointing my camera towards nature, and more often than not, the camera will capture an orb. Once, Archangel Michael's blue wings could be seen as a blue light as he stood behind a friend. I have been shown digital photographs taken on mobile phones of angels, and two of those were breathtaking. The first was of Archangel Michael holding his sword standing outside a club in Sydney, protecting it. The second photo was an angel imprinted against the morning dew on a window. These photos were not wishy-washy, 'maybe-they-are, maybe-they're-not' type of photo; they were extremely clear. Often when taking digital photos of a group of like-minded Earth Angels you will capture orbs, unexplained lights and mists. I used to think these photos were duds, but I view them very differently these days, because I know the angels are in the photos. As we were walking along a path at the Coolum Resort on the last evening of Doreen's course we saw a few women looking up at an owl in a tree. As I began taking photographs I noticed with amazement there was not one owl, but four!

The one key aspect for me during my ongoing learning at my University of Intuition has been the angels and meditation. Meditation has been the key to unlocking any fears or doubts. It opens your intuition. I had been advised for years to meditate but I resisted, thinking I could not do it or that it would take too long to do. I found that guided visualization meditations were a great place to start, before moving into my own meditation practice of breathing and relaxation. Once you get into a rhythm of meditating daily you will find that the doors to your intuition will open and you will not only be welcoming the angels into your life, but you will be surrounded by a peace and tranquility that will radiate out into your everyday life. The *angels will be in your mist,* just as they were in my photos.

Beginners 10 Minute Meditation

Meditation is very serene, calming and relaxing and helps to open up your intuition. Whether you have 10 minutes or 1 hour to enjoy the benefits related to meditation, time is not the key . . . breath is.

This beginner's meditation and breathing technique can be done anywhere or anytime. Find yourself a comfortable place where you won't be disturbed. Maybe resting on your bed, or under a tree, or even sitting in a chair. It does not matter what you wear or what you look like; comfort is key here.

Some people find that soft meditative music playing in the background helps them relax and gives them something to focus on as they breathe. Choose a piece of music that is about 10 minutes long to start with. Choosing relaxing music of a set length of time will allow you to relax into your meditation without worrying how long you have left. As you progress with your daily practice of meditation, you can extend the time if you wish, or meditate more often.

Find the position you want to meditate in; make yourself comfortable, relax your body, and place your hands on your belly with your fingertips just touching each other. Close your eyes and inhale deeply through your nose all the way down to your belly. As your belly expands, your fingertips will gently separate and this will let you know that your breath is right down in your belly.

If you find it hard to take a deep breath, imagine bypassing the lungs and you will find the breath goes straight down to the belly. As you exhale, release the air through your mouth. If you find it more relaxing, you can exhale through your nose. As your belly flattens on the out breath, you will know you are breathing correctly when your fingertipss touch together again. As you continue deep breathing, imagine your body relaxing, starting with your toes and working your way up through your body to the top of your head with each outgoing breath.

Now with each in-breath, count to four. Breathe in – one and two and three and four. Hold the breath for a count of four – one and two and three and four. Release the breath for a count of four – breathing out, one and two and three and four. Hold the breath for a count of four – one and two and three and four. Continue this breathing rhythm throughout the meditation. You will find that once you have practiced a few meditations you will no longer need to count or to feel your fingertips; it will flow naturally for you. You can change the rhythm to a breath of 6 to 3, or try 4 to 2 if this feels more comfortable.

If you have never breathed deeply and slowly before, you may perhaps start to feel lightheaded. Wait a few minutes whilst breathing normally before you try the slow and deep breathing again. You could also try breathing less deeply.

If any thoughts come into your mind, acknowledge them and release them on the out breath. Keep coming back to your breathing. Your focus is on the breath; you are learning the basic breathing techniques of meditation. Let any thoughts come and go and breathe them out of your mind on the out breath.

As the meditation comes to a close, gently bring your attention back to yourself and your surroundings. Become aware of your body and gently move your fingers and toes; stretch and open your eyes. Ensure that you center yourself by being fully aware of your body in its surrounds before standing up. Keep yourself hydrated by drinking a glass of water as required.

Try to meditate for 10 minutes each day. Morning and night is optimal when learning, however meditating once a week is better than not meditating at all. You can even meditate first thing in the morning or last thing at night whilst you are lying in bed. It is a great way to commence your day and an even calmer way to end it.

～

Safe Haven

*Your angels are helping you to discover
an inner sanctuary of peace and
tranquility.*

*When you take time out to rest
and nourish your physical, emotional
and spiritual self, you create a safe
haven for your soul. You may draw on
the well-spring of this inner sanctuary
at any time for inspiration
and guidance, for it is here that
heaven and earth meet.*

ROBYN RIDLEY
Wagga Wagga, NSW, Australia

ROBYN RIDLEY has worked in the health and healing fields for more than fifteen years. She has a Bachelor of Nursing and a Graduate Certificate in Advanced Clinical Nursing. Robyn is currently employed as a part-time clinical nurse specialist in the field of sexual and reproductive health. In addition to this, she has a Diploma in Metaphysics from the International Academy of Vibrational Therapies and works and teaches in the healing and metaphysical fields. She is a Reiki master/teacher of Reiki/Seichim and Complimentary Therapy Practitioner. Robyn has completed the Angel Intuitive™ with Advanced Training and the Angel Therapy® Mediumship Training certified by Doreen Virtue, PhD.

Robyn is also an Aura-Soma® colour care consultant, teacher and beamer light pen practitioner. It was her passion for colour and crystals that led her on this awesome spiritual journey through the Aura-Soma® colour care system, crystal therapy, Zenith Omega™, Seraphim Healing, and varying other vibrational healing modalities. More recently Robyn has become a registered massage therapist with a keen interest in Lomi Lomi Massage.

Robyn prides herself in helping others become more empowered and she does this through consultations, teaching and organizing workshops and retreats.

Robyn has also conducted research for Dr Doreen Virtue and contributed to Louise L. Hay's book entitled Modern-Day Miracles. She is now working on her forthcoming book, *Loving the Essence* and deck of *Ancient Healing Oracle* cards.

Robyn can be contacted through the Crystal Clear Reflections website at www.crystalclearreflections.com.au.

Connecting with the Goddess Within

ROBYN RIDLEY

*We travel through the endless corridors of our mind until
one day we find a pathway that leads to our heart.*

—SALERNO

fter my mother died, I had a visitation from her telling me everything was
all right. She appeared at the foot of my bed and said to me, "I'm okay."
I had to pinch myself to see if I was dreaming . . . No, I wasn't. Mum appeared
looking the way she normally looked – a middle aged woman, smartly dressed
with a quirky but reassuring smile on her face. It was like she was cocooned in
an aura of light supported by the angels, and this took away her sharp defining
features.

She must have known that I needed to hear those words. At the time I felt like
my life was in tatters. What was life all about? I was on a journey where I had no
control, not even of myself. When Mum appeared I was taken by surprise but I felt
her warmth in my heart. How important it was for me to hear her speak those
words, to feel her presence once again and more importantly, to know that she
cared! I felt all alone in the world, a feeling I had experienced quite deeply once
before, and in fact, was still experiencing.

Her reassuring gaze reinforced the fact that I wasn't alone. But on a physical
level this feeling of being alone was so overwhelming that it engulfed me at times.
I wanted to feel her hug, but knowing that I would never feel this again was heart-
wrenching – it tore me apart. I hated grief. I hated feeling responsible; I hated
feeling guilty not only about all that had gone wrong in my life, but about the
feeling that I had lost control.

As an only child I grieved. My children who were obviously the apple of her
eye grieved. My husband, having connected to my mother as his own was grieving, and my father who was now living with us also grieved. I cried myself to sleep
many a night. It just didn't seem fair that she should be taken from us. She was
such a selfless woman, one who gave to everyone, and now she was gone. Such a
void! A part of me felt guilty because I was looking at her death from the view-
point of what it was we were losing. This seemed so much the opposite of what

she was like. I felt selfish – not selfless. I asked myself the question – can I go through this again?

It was almost the full term pregnancy that I had planned. It was awesome. I was finally having a child that I so desperately wanted! My life had just begun to fall into place and everything seemed perfect. Well almost. I remember having a 'show' indicating that I might be going into labor – "Yes!" I yelled. This was my first natural birth, having had two inductions previously. It was a dream of mine to have a natural childbirth with no intervention. I was so excited and felt reassured because that afternoon I had an appointment with my doctor. A friend drove me 30 minutes to my appointment because by this stage I was beginning to have minor contractions.

Arriving at the doctor's office for my check-up, I informed him that I had had a 'show' and he looked at me and said "Is that good?" Checking my dates he said "Yes it is." It was then and only then that I told him of my concerns that I hadn't felt the baby move for a few days – not since Saturday night in fact, and it was now Tuesday. He asked me to climb onto the examination couch so he could use the hand-held device to listen to the baby's heart beat. Oh dread! Just as I had secretly feared but didn't want to face – there was no heart beat. How can this be? What does this mean? I didn't want to know.

Oh God, if ever there was a time that I wished I wasn't intuitive and in touch with my body it was now. I wanted to run and hide; I wanted to die; I wanted to scream and yell. This can't be happening! I remember proceeding to the hospital for an ultrasound – a scan that showed absolutely nothing. How can this be? I was almost full term with a huge tummy so vividly displaying a baby inside . . . What am I going to do? How am I going to tell anyone? My worst nightmare . . . I felt like a total failure as a woman, as a mother and as a wife.

I had to walk and walk around the hospital to further progress the labor that had started naturally. My friend accompanied me and to this day I remember making jokes and trying to pretend nothing had happened. We walked, talked, laughed and occasionally cried. I phoned my husband to come to the hospital and informed him of the death of the baby. In a sense he was in denial. Because of his work, I sent him home late that evening because the labor would go on for a few more hours and it was getting very late. I should have known that I would give birth sooner than expected. I went into the labor room alone and gave birth to my beautiful baby girl. I held her to my breast as any mother would. She was perfect. I was expecting something far from perfect and in all her perfection my heart went out to her. She was beautiful, with her father's and sister's top lip, her arm so soft and her skin free from any blemishes.

There was an overwhelming sense of love in the room followed by an over-whelming sense of grief. The doctor and nurse on duty had never been in the room with a mother and her stillborn baby. I wanted to hold her forever; I can still feel and see her soft subtle skin. How could something so perfect be taken from me forever? Though no photos were taken, I know that nothing can replace that vivid memory in my mind. And yet I knew that nobody else would ever understand, and for this too I was angry and resentful. I cried when they took her from me. I wanted to dress her; I wanted to hold her, and I wanted her to be alive . . . At this point it seemed like there was absolutely nothing fair in this world. All power had been taken away from me, or so it seemed.

Life continues as usual – or does it? I had no idea how to cope. I hated myself as a mother, wife and ultimately as a woman. I felt that I had failed . . . Where to go from here? How does one learn to cope and deal with such things? I could only believe that my little girl that I had felt growing inside me was an angel herself. Surely this is not the end. If ever I believed in angels, now was the time. Having had many intuitive and clairvoyant experiences throughout my life, even as I went into labor with Karinda-Lee, I knew that there was something much greater out there.

This didn't numb the pain. I really craved to be loved; I wanted attention; I didn't want to feel alone. I wanted to have fun and carry on with life without really taking the time to go within. I began drinking excessively. It seemed that when I drank it would temporarily take away any aches and pains, and even if for brief moments it could bring me pleasure and power, albeit not real. Unfortunately, the effects of drinking too much meant that I wasn't there for my other two children as I could have been, or for my husband.

During my childhood and teenage years I was in a home where my father obviously drank way too much. I resented this, even to the point that I was disappointed when my mother didn't leave him. Here I was now turning to alcohol myself not really caring about the impact it was having on myself, or those around me. I was angry within and without. I would lash out at others and I would turn the anger on myself. I hated who and what I was becoming. Who was I now? I was someone who was all alone, had terrible coping skills, and someone who despite appearances, was dreadfully unhappy.

The grief of losing my mother was intense, but it was at this time that I was forced to look at things differently. I had to believe that there was something else. Life just couldn't end there. If that were the case then what would be the purpose? I know my mother touched the lives of many and my beautiful baby daughter touched me to the depths like no other. I was experiencing the pain of losing the love and connection between a mother and child – both as a mother and as a child. This was a huge learning curve for me. What I had to accept was the fact that life does go on. I had a lovely husband and two beautiful children, and it was time to bring the focus back to them.

My son was devastated following the loss of his sister and grandmother, and though my daughter was very young, she was not untouched by this immense grief. It became obvious to me as my daughter grew older that she was reflecting back to me my own pain of being a woman. She was a beautiful free spirit and ever so forgiving. Unfortunately I took advantage of this and probably picked on her the most. Can the pain of losing one child impact on the love delivered to another? Can a mother who feels so trapped resent the freedom expressed by her own daughter? It seemed that I was beginning to reflect back how my mother so readily accepted abuse. We shared the same fears. I too have stayed in a situation where I wasn't happy for fear of being alone. Yet upon losing both my mother and my daughter I got to experience the ultimate aloneness.

My mother and daughter were earth angels. That is unquestionable and I believe that their purpose continues on the other side. A lot of personal reflection followed their loss, not always positive but intense nonetheless. Having lost two of the three most important females in my life, I really had to look at my own feminine aspect. My feelings towards my femininity were bound up in a continuous and destructive battle with my weight -constantly trying to lose it, only to regain it. I really did not want it any longer. This struggle went on for many years.

Self Acceptance

You are perfect, whole and complete, just as you are.

Your angels guide you to let go of any negative self-judgments and see yourself through their eyes. They love and accept you unconditionally, and ask that you see and love yourself just as they do.

"Don't eat that or you'll get fat" was a common theme for discussion around eating for me as a child. I'd already learned by the early age of nine or ten that eating led to becoming fat. Being an only child I was often left alone, and after work Mum would take me to the shop for an ice-cream or chips. I felt this was our bonding time, walking to the shop and back. It made me feel special because I was being given something I liked. Though I loved the treats, when the comments about my weight started coming I felt ashamed and sad about my body, even though I was still very young. As a teenager I began to look at myself differently. I wanted to be liked, so I put myself on diets. This led me to looking in the mirror and actually liking what I saw. I wanted to be popular rather than the 'fat' one. Boys did like me, though I thought that all the other girls were much prettier.

When I shed some weight and bought new clothes I had a greater sense of self. I was connecting with the Goddess, albeit young, youthful and naive. There even came a point in my life where I felt gorgeous. But I didn't really know what to do with this beauty; I didn't really believe it on one level, having taken in all the comments from the past. It didn't take long to become confused around popularity, sexuality and sensuality. These were all linked, but I had no idea how I was meant to act. I had a long list of *shoulds* and *shouldn'ts* and given my Catholic upbringing, the guilt that went along with exploration of sexuality. It was total confusion.

I wanted to look womanly and beautiful, but wasn't sure this was acceptable. I wanted to fit in but at what cost? I had my own set of moral standards that were impossibly high, so I felt completely lost. My father would have loved a son I'm sure, and part of me felt sad about this. Ultimately I just never felt good enough. In a sense I had begun to equate masculinity with power, and as a female I wanted to be powerful, yet questioned whether this was acceptable.

Now as an adult, it was time to delve in and look at this void in my life, to really look at what was happening for me. I perceived myself as having a masculine appearance, though many people wouldn't believe it when I told them. I felt a real aversion to looking like a man. People would say to me, "You are so womanly; how can you possibly think that?" It was when one woman in a healing group asked the others not to comment but rather acknowledge that this was how I was feeling, that I finally felt I was being heard without judgment. That was such a special moment, to have my true feelings acknowledged. I really began to search then, not only into why I had an aversion to perceiving myself that way, but also into what the issues were surrounding that.

I remember standing in front of the mirror, trying to get my hair just right and my makeup perfect. I had curves, wore makeup and miniskirts. You can't get much more feminine than that so I really had to tackle this head on. I would stand there and cry, knowing that no one would or could understand. I didn't feel pretty enough; I didn't feel womanly enough; I didn't feel whole or complete. Standing there and knowing that there was a huge void within me was so sad. I loathed myself; I loathed my past; I loathed all that I had become, and for what reason I was never quite certain.

My daughter was maturing into a lovely young woman by this time, and whilst it was lovely watching her blossom, I was resentful that I had lost all opportunity of feeling beautiful myself. Her freedom never ceased to amaze me, something I feel that I missed as a child. My daughter was always the one who told me I was beautiful. I used to wonder how she could see that as I often used her as a scapegoat. Maybe I was rejecting any love that was coming towards me, because I certainly didn't know how to give it to myself. I felt ugly, fat and not good enough, and sometimes I just felt sick looking in the mirror. In hindsight I'm sure I drew to me the type of people who would reflect these aspects back to me. I couldn't go on like this anymore! I needed to continue exploring in depth the old feelings of shame, guilt, worthlessness, and those feelings of being unlovable, because I wanted to finally release that ugly beast within me.

I started with mirror work as recommended by Louise Hay. I had to tell myself positive things in the mirror and say positive things about myself, even if I didn't believe them. It was like "Fake it till you make it." When I began to read about the abuse that the author Denise Linn encountered, this prompted me to look at my own abuse and how this had impacted on my own life. Denise's book, *The Glory and Pleasure of being a Woman* reminded me of the Goddess within. Whilst

I could see the Goddess at times, I couldn't embrace her. Yet both of these women encouraged me to look at my own body, to explore it and to love it. This was very difficult at first, but when I took everyone else out of the equation I became much more empowered. I had spent too much time worrying about what others thought of me rather than embracing myself.

At last I entered a time in my life of re-connecting to my spiritual being through various healing modalities, the first being the Aura-Soma® colour care system. It was amazing how much colour taught me about myself. I often had dreams showing me the truth . . . and nightmares looking at my shadow self, including anger, the monster and the devil archetypes. These were also accompanied by dreams of beauty, including my own radiance, my shining light, my deep inner wisdom and ultimate knowing. Once when I began to experience panic attacks, I was fortunate to uncover new ways to overcome this. It was time to take responsibility and in a sense get back in the driver's seat. One colleague pointed out to me that I often rejected things before they could reject me – talk about a sledgehammer! But it was these truths about myself that initiated change. I may not have wanted to hear this but I did listen and it was ever so powerful. I realized that I gave too much of myself and that I needed to bring the focus back to me. My crystals also assisted me in this process on my healing journey.

It was through meditation, dreams and healings that I accessed past lives, showing me where I'd previously failed and how and why I'd feared being alone. I am aware that some people don't believe in past lives but it is upon looking at these influences that I have been able to draw on those strengths and apply them currently. Reiki and meditation enabled me to connect to past issues and heal them. I remember being horrified when my eyes were covered on the Reiki table. This brought about fear from deep within. It took me back to childhood abuse, and whilst this was painful at the time, it was a catalyst for me to make changes now, with awareness. I realized for the first time in my life that I was beautiful, and anything that had happened in my past is now in my past, and that I have the power to create a new life based on all my learned experiences.

In recent years, courses in metaphysics, clairvoyance, mediumship and angels have enabled me to tap into my intuitive side. Through this, and connecting with the angels, spirit and the Divine, I have been able to see, hear and feel the truth. I can honestly say now that I have a deeper understanding of the Goddess within than I ever thought possible.

The angels assisted me on my weight loss journey through instruction, direction, meditation, and motivation. However, this was only a symptom of my connecting on a deeper level to my very essence. The Archangels, the Ascended Masters, who are beings of wisdom that have ascended following completion of their works here on earth, and some of the many Gods and Goddesses have assisted me on my journey through direction, guidance, comfort and connection with my soul purpose.

If you find yourself questioning your inner or outer beauty, don't forget to call on the angels who are waiting in the wings, readily available. It's important to know that they are all there to assist us, if we will only ask. You can read more about the qualities of the Archangels and Ascended Masters in *Archangels & Ascended Masters*, by Doreen Virtue, Ph.D., or *The Aura-Soma Sourcebook*, by Mike Booth with Carol McKnight. I also encourage you to meditate, converse and consult with the angels, archangels, ascended masters and various Gods and Goddesses on a personal level, as this is far more rewarding than simply reading about them, and can have a far greater impact on your life.

In my own journey, I wasn't always in a place where I was ready to ask for their assistance, but now I know that it is my right, just as it is yours. If you've ever doubted yourself or had any questions that need answering, know that you're not alone and that you are one hundred percent supported by these heavenly beings!

Through teaching and working alongside others in the healing professions, I know that it is because of our personal experience that we can offer compassion and understanding to our clients. My aim is to assist others to become empowered, especially through connecting or re-connecting to the God or Goddess within. What excites me now is that I am no longer focused on my weight, but rather on how I'm feeling within myself. When I am connected to my center and feeling balanced, the scales no longer rule my life, as they had in the past. I no longer look in the mirror and dislike what I see, and I no longer live my life to please those around me. Rather, I'm living life for myself and on purpose, which totally fills that void that had been ever-present in my earlier years.

Today, I am the Goddess. I am proud of my femininity and I encourage you and all the women in your life to connect with the Goddess within.

Connecting with the Goddess Within – Affirmations and Meditation
Take the time to stand or sit in front of the mirror. Look deeply into your eyes as they are the mirror to your soul. Acknowledge those aspects of yourself that you may not be happy with and allow yourself to feel what is happening right now for you. You may feel a little uncomfortable. You might feel sad, or happy. Just recognize or identify who you are right now. It's time now to give yourself the recognition that you deserve.

> ***Affirm to yourself that you are an awesome being***
> ***and that you are so deserving of Love!***

Spend a little time each day saying at least one positive thing to yourself. Now take the time to experience your truth.

Find a place where you feel comfortable and allow yourself to relax, gently closing your eyes if you feel comfortable. Take three slow deep breaths – breathing in peace and breathing out anything that no longer serves you. It's time now to call in the Angels, Ascended Masters, Gods and Goddesses and anyone else who you feel can assist you.

Ask the angels to assist you to feel whole and complete. Connect with the feeling of compassion. You are totally loved right now and the angels are showing you the benefits of you showing compassion to yourself, not just to those around you. Now, connect with your warrior self. Tap into your power center and feel that you are awesome, just the way you are. The angels and all those around you in spirit are showering you with abundance. Feel and embrace that sense of abundance – you are not lacking anything. Throughout this experience, allow any feelings to surface. If thoughts come into your mind, just allow them to come and go.

I want you now to take a deep, healing breath and feel yourself surrounded by Angelic Crystalline energy. This is the energy of clear quartz, programmed with angelic love. Allow the energy of the angels and the crystals to clear your energy fields on all levels. Imagine this gentle clear quartz and angelic energy inside your body, and throughout your auric field around the outside of your body. If you feel that there is anyone you need to release who is preventing you from standing in your power, then imagine the energy coming from a pointy clear quartz laser crystal and cutting through the cord that is connecting you and this other person or event. Take a moment to feel your freedom. Take the time to feel what your energy is like in its purest form. You are perfect just the way you are! Feel your wholeness; feel your sense of self expanding and know that you don't need anything more than what you have right now. Take a little time to sit in this space . . .

When you are ready, bring your attention back to your heart center and take a deep breath. As you awaken and open your eyes, smile with gratitude as you accept and reinforce each and every aspect of your Inner Goddess and purest self.

Go Forth in Love . . .

❧

Bibliography

Salerno, T. *Gaia Body and Soul*. Blue Angel Gallery, 2007.
Hay, Louise, L. *You Can Heal Your Life*. Hay House, 1999.
Linn, Denise. *Secrets and Mysteries*. Hay House, 2002.

Compassion

Your angels ask that you have compassion for everyone, including yourself.

Let go of any struggle in your life. Be extra gentle with yourself, surrendering the situation to your angels. Where there was frustration or hurt, let it go. By releasing any unforgiveness of yourself and others, you allow the angels to open your heart to more loving solutions.

ORIETTA MAMMARELLA

Melbourne, Victoria, Australia

ORIETTA MAMMARELLA was born aware of the angelic realms and this has led her on a lifetime journey of self discovery. Though she worked for many years in customer service roles in complaint handling and conciliation for the private and public sectors, she always yearned to really help people on a deep, soul level and to become self employed. After participating in various healing studies, Orietta is now a practitioner of Reiki, Essence of Angels, and an Angel Intuitive™ certified by Doreen Virtue Ph D. Since leaving the corporate world, Orietta is self employed in her own business, Celestial Heart.

Orietta has developed her own personal healing technique utilizing a combination of Reiki, Archangel and Spirit Guide channeling along with vocal chakra vibrational toning to aid her clients to reach their full potential to heal mind, body and soul. She strongly believes in empowering others by teaching them to heal themselves. When one heals, one heals the world around them, therefore creating peace, love and happiness.

Orietta lives in the northern suburbs of Melbourne with her husband, daughter and two dogs, Leia and Sasha. She is currently enjoying motherhood and her daughter's activities, plunging into her passion for writing and studying for a degree in Naturopathy.

If you would like to experience a session with Orietta or learn more about Orietta's upcoming workshops and meditations, please visit her at her website www.celestialheart.com.au

Angelic Butterfly:
From Guiding Angel to New Earth Child

ORIETTA MAMMARELLA

Although I was born open to the invisible realms, God and the angels will only show and teach me what my human form can handle.

It was mid morning on a lazy summer's day as I gazed out my window, sinking into a peaceful meditation. Daydreaming is where my creative ideas and dreams manifest. Smiling, I was remembering my childlike innocence and wisdom during an incident in the third grade. A teacher described on my report card that my issue was that I frequently daydreamed. Up until that time I thought it was normal to stare out the window and look for my fairy friends. As a sensitive child, the thought that my daydreaming was seen as wrong was hurtful. I wondered whether the teacher understood that daydreaming is where our creativity has a chance to enter our soul and fill us with remembrance that life is truly magical, and is meant to be lived in joy.

Sighing deeply, I then thought about when I consciously began talking to the angels for the first time. No one taught me how to connect with these celestial beings, yet I have always felt their guiding light. In a hypnotized and relaxed state, staring out the living room window, I felt a tap on my shoulder. As I breathed deeply and filled my body with oxygen, I felt two little angels curling themselves up on my lap.

To my astonishment I heard them sing, "Hi Mom!" The female looked about eight years old and the little boy around five. Both were wearing night gowns typically fashionable of the late 1800's era. "We are your future children," the dominant female stated. "You and Dad will meet and I will be born in around 10 year's time." The little boy was so bashful that he hid behind his sister.

"We love you very much and I will be just as cheeky as you were as a child." She then went on to explain that we had lived together before, though last time they had died in a house fire. She didn't explain any more than I needed to know at that time. Although I was born open to the invisible realms, God and the angels will only show and teach me what my human form can handle. It was many years later while I was quietly meditating that I saw the full extent on how my spirit children had died in a previous lifetime.

My own childhood was typical of a first generation migrant. I was an Italian-Australian Catholic, growing up in a neighborhood where everybody had relatives overseas and everyone spoke a second language. Housework was done on Saturdays, our Moms and Grandmas could out-cook celebrity chefs any day, and we played soccer in the street with the neighborhood kids. We all had a backyard full of vegetables, chickens, fruit trees and a lawn for the dog to do his business. Our front yards contained perfumed flowers, mainly roses and carnations. Carnations are sturdy enough to be placed on our deceased relative's cemetery plots.

The front and back yards were magical kingdoms. There by the Banksia plant lived the gumnut fairy. This tree was significant as it was given to my parents at their citizenship. Down by the daffodils and carnations lived my fairy friends. They would dare me to wet my parents with a garden hose while watering the garden.

Oftentimes, my fairy and angel friends would wake me in the morning as a kaleidoscope of golden orbs displayed a bouncing light show in my room. While everyone in my house was still asleep I would crawl out and try to step on my friends. Stomp, stomp, stomp and giggle, as I could never catch them. A child's world is a magical kingdom. Even on grey rainy days, children can see the beauty and magic in the rain.

As a sensitive child, when I was very distressed and felt the world was a harsh place to be, my crying would suddenly stop. I would feel oozing warmth spreading within my being and a deep knowing that Mother Mary and a legion of angels were by my side. I felt hands on my head and shoulders, bringing an instant calm and a feeling of deep inner peace. Now into my adulthood, my guiding angels have taught me healing and meditation techniques, explained sacred sites and imparted clues to my spiritual development.

It was no surprise when ten years after my angel children visited me that summer morning, I was informed through a vision that an impending pregnancy was forthcoming. The child would be in a body soon and would like a name beginning with "S." It wasn't long after this message that I fell pregnant. The year leading up to when I realized I was pregnant was filled with deep stress, loss and awakening.

When death comes knocking on a relatives' door, Archangel Azrael, known as the angel of death, endings and beginnings, shows himself to me through dreams and visions. One particular evening, Azrael presented himself with my Great Grandmother and I was shown a very long table under an ancient olive tree, filled with an abundance of home-cooked Italian food and trimmings. All of my deceased relatives were seated at the table. My Great Grandmother, as host, informed me that they were awaiting the King. I knew it was time; Nonno (Grandfather) would be crossing over soon.

That weekend I was in a Reiki workshop and the angels were by my side holding my hand and soothing me. Little did I know that by that afternoon I would have the last physical eye contact with Nonno before he went into a coma.

My family and I waited five long days for him to go to the light and reconnect with God. We would coax him, telling him it was OK to cross over and leave his body behind. In the meantime, the World Cup football tournament was happening and Australia's *Socceroos* were doing very well. Coming from a family of soccer fanatics, the World Cup is always a huge event. Having Italian ancestry meant we always went for the Italian team, *Il Azzuri*, but in 2006 the air was different. Our beloved country, Australia, made it to the most important and most-watched sporting event in the world.

The night Nonno died was particularly eerie. Italy and Australia were playing for their Round 8 placement. Italy's match was first and this game began close to midnight.

Up until that point I was suffering from fatigue, hunger and all the symptoms associated with the early stages of pregnancy. That evening before I said goodbye to Nonno, Archangel Azrael informed me to do a Reiki treatment. Nonno was suffering the effects of morphine and other drugs and couldn't find the light to cross over. This treatment helped his spirit look for the bridge to cross over into the light. I knew the next time I would see him he would be in spirit.

As I lay in bed trying to sleep I heard my husband cheering on as Italy kicked a goal that would confirm their place in Round 8. It was 12.35am. I felt Archangel Azrael beside me. I knew in my heart that the King

> ## Children
>
> *Your inner child is just as important to nurture as the children in your life.*
>
> *All children need to feel acknowledged and loved, lighthearted and carefree. Take time out to play, laugh and have fun as you care for the children in your life, and the child within you.*

had just died and I sure knew that Italy would win the world cup that year. You see, waiting on the other side was Nonno's son, who died of cancer twelve years before. My uncle played local soccer league and was crazy for the sport. When Italy scored, I thought of Uncle Tory and I just knew Nonno had crossed over.

Sure enough the phone rang, confirming that Nonno died at 12.36pm. We all went back to the hospital to say our goodbyes. By the time we got back home, Australia's match was on. Needless to say our grief was strong, but who was able to sleep that night? I later learnt that the entire family watched the Australian Socceroos on TV. I think we all felt that the angels spoke to us through sport and as weird as it sounds, Italy's score at the time of Nonno's death reminded us of our beloved Tory. Our angels work in symbolism, and I believe we all felt this in those early hours of the morning.

Fatigue finally set in and sleep was upon us. Just before day break, I placed my hands on my tummy and exhaled as I had learnt in yoga class. It was then that I felt a very strong pulse in my tummy and I realized I was pregnant. During that day, I received confirmation through a home test kit that I was indeed expecting. The day Nonno died was the day I discovered I was having a baby.

Our two favorite teams played against each other in Round 8 for a place in the quarter finals, and Italy beat Australia, though the Australian media criticized it as unfair. I was happy that Italy had won as it's the land where Nonno and my ancestors were born. As most of us know, Italy did win the 2006 Football World Cup. It wasn't a surprise! The angels hinted that this was going to happen.

At eight weeks of pregnancy, I was on the train going to work, daydreaming and looking at my reflection in the window. I felt something like a pop in my energy field and then a tap on my shoulder. "Hi Mom!" It was my little boy. I said to him, "What are you doing out there? Why aren't you in my womb?" I was oblivious as to what communicating to this little angel outside the womb really meant. He then said many times that he loved me, that he was OK and that everything would be OK.

That night I dreamt of Nonno. He was holding a photo frame that depicted a decorated border of toys and a title stating 'It's a boy.' The photo was of a black void. Still in dreamtime, I was curious as to why I couldn't see the baby. Since childhood I would dream of deceased relatives and angels. I learnt very early on that when I have these dreams, it's important to pay attention, as it's a message for me or somebody I know.

My nightmare began when at ten and half weeks I had unusual symptoms. The ultrasound revealed a black picture just like I dreamt. The photo was of a black void! My little boy was gone! No heart beat, no shape, nothing. I was informed the pregnancy ended around eight weeks. I would say it ended during that time on the train, as I clearly remember feeling a strange 'pop' sensation.

I couldn't believe it! I had a deep connection with this soul. I remember thinking it was strange at the time, that the little boy was with me because, ten years before they said that the girl would be born first. The morning that I was required to go to hospital for a curette, Nonno's spirit and that of Archangel Raphael, the angel of healing, and Mother Mary were beside me. The angels were cloaking me with their love just like they did when I was a child. An immense warmth surrounded my body, like the feeling one has when wrapped in their favorite blanket.

As I was about to go into surgery, I felt Archangel Raphael holding my hand relaying profound words of wisdom, that I was already healed. I then feel Nonno next to me and his angelic words made my eyes well up. "I am by your side, dear child, holding your hand like you were by my side when I was struggling to find the light. I thank you for helping me and making me feel comfortable when I crossed over. I heard your words and now I am here doing the same for you, holding your hand and comforting you."

Needless to say, the surgical nurse, Anne-Marie, saw my emotional state and she was crying with me. I shared my thoughts with her, explaining that the angels were with me. The compassionate tears I saw within her warmed my heart, woman to woman, healer to healer. We understood each other. I thanked God and the angels for bringing Anne-Marie to me during the operation. They wheeled me into surgery and the angels had another surprise for me. As I was going under the anesthetic, I heard the song from Andrea Bocelli, *Time to Say Goodbye*, from what seemed like the loud speaker.

> " . . . Con te partiro (*With you I will leave*)
> Su navi per mari (*On ships across seas*)
> Che io lo so (*Which, I know*)
> No no non esistono piu (*No, no, exist no longer*)
> Con te partiro (*With you I will leave*) . . . "

In those ten weeks I felt the joy and unconditional love that one feels for their child. For a short moment I knew what it was like to be a mother. I also discovered that my unborn baby had a soul.

The doctors suggested naming our baby and performing a prayer ceremony. We named him Samuelle and during our prayer ceremony he communicated a message of hope. He said that the miscarriage was destined as a balance of karma between us. He needed to gently come back on the earth plane as he is very sensitive to the harshness of this reality.

This miscarriage had strengthened my will and purpose on the earth. I felt empowered to remember what it feels like to be a mother. There was the strength of fire inside of me. I felt tall and I felt like nothing could hurt me. I also learnt something new, that a soul *does* come through in the early weeks. For the time being, I just needed to heal.

Two months after this ordeal, I became pregnant again but nature provided another shock. It was an ectopic pregnancy which could prove fatal if left untreated. To save my fallopian tube, I was administered a chemotherapy drug that kills off the pregnancy cells.

When the all-clear was given, I fell into the depths of despair. Depression crept up slowly and ate away at my heart. The feeling of being a mother but not able to fulfill my longing was excruciating.

Slowly I found strength and courage by spending time in nature. I poured my heart out to the goddess of the ocean. I felt Mother Nature kiss me in the face and wipe away my tears. I felt my heart open and faith entered as I believe that God and my angels were beckoning me to heal.

One winter afternoon, Archangel Azrael tapped me on my shoulder. He had been trying to get my attention all day and so I gave in to the angelic presence. I centered myself by taking three breaths and quickly called on Archangel Michael to protect the impending communication. Archangel Azrael said that I would finally receive an answer to my curiosity about what it feels and looks like when a soul is born on the earth plane.

Then I saw the scene of the other side, with the huge olive tree. But this time there was no long festive table. There present were both my husband's and my own deceased grandmothers and behind them, our family lineage. My angel daughter and Samuelle stood in front of the grandmothers. They were all saying goodbye to this daughter. She looked about 12 years old, as if she had grown up in spirit. She was wearing her traveling clothes and held a brown suitcase. The grandmothers were fretting about her just like a typical mother figure would.

She was approaching a bridge which she was about to cross over. A gentle running stream divided us from the other world and this bridge crossed over that stream. At the foot of the small bridge, Samuelle ran over to her for one last warm hug. He also looked like he had grown up in spirit. He was so happy to see her go and reassured her that all would be OK. Everyone had proud tears of joy to see her off. It felt like that time my family bid farewell to me as I was about to board a plane to Europe. She was about to cross over when Grandmother Grace hastily cried, "Don't forget that the keys are held in the suitcase. Don't forget to look in your suitcase!" The child looked back one more time, waved farewell, took a deep breath of anticipation, filled with excitement and enthusiasm, and then crossed over.

She was flying through wormholes, space, stars, galaxies far, far, away. Everything around her was a blur and faster than the speed of light. She was traveling through time, universes and different realities, to be on this earth plane. It was such a beautiful vision that I held back tears and had trouble focusing so as not to black out. Finally her journey slowed down to earth time and the vision ended in my tummy region, until it was a diminished bright star, and into a metamorphosis of a pulse in a warm, underwater cocoon. I came to my senses; I had just witnessed the opposite of death. I think I just conceived. By the end of that week I had nausea and by two weeks after this vision the home pregnancy kit showed that I was pregnant, again.

During this whole ordeal with child bearing I came to witness that not only do angels exist in spirit form but also in the form of humans. I was in labor on a day that Melbourne experienced severe storms which caused many blackouts including the hospital I was in.

The storm was raging outside and I could see through the windows huge pine trees swaying in hurricane-like winds. After concentrating for seven hours on hypno-birthing, a natural pain relief breathing technique for childbirth, I then lost control and allowed fear to enter my being. The fear of destructive wind entered my senses and the echo of death was surrounding my aura. My parents visited me to see how I was faring. In the midst of my birth pain and eager for an epidural, I saw the foreboding look of grief on their faces. Even in the midst of labor I could read and feel the opening vibrations of the other side.

Late that afternoon there was a midwife shift change. A kind-hearted midwife introduced herself as Anne-Marie. With gleaming eyes and heartfelt gratitude she said that it was a blessing to be with me on this day, and to see me come full circle. She said that there are some patients who stood out for her and I was one of them. She was the nurse crying with me as I was about to go into surgery after the miscarriage. This time she was there for me, assisting me in the birth of my child. This was a sign and blessing from the angels!

Just before my child was born, I experienced what doctors call hallucinations, but what I call the opening of deep feminine intuition. I was mumbling all sorts of visions I saw about my daughter and the unsettledness we were going to experience in the following year. Sara Lily was finally born at 10 past midnight, all wise and knowing in her jaundiced eyes.

The following day I was given a gift that left me speechless. It was a photo frame like in that dream long ago, but instead it was titled, "It's a girl!" I was also informed that a very dear family friend passed away during the howling of that wind and the moment that I lost concentration for a drug-free birth.

Sara's unsettledness was challenging. In the wee hours of one particular morning Archangel Metatron introduced himself to me, gently whispering instructions on how to help her. He created a soothing and nurturing feeling, clearing the energies in her room together with Archangel Michael. Sara, my husband and I have had better sleep since then. I believe Metatron also helps parents raising an indigo or crystal child to be authentic in their decision making and techniques. I have nicknamed Metatron the "super nanny."

Recently, I was reminded of my childhood when through a camera surveillance I saw the same display of bouncing golden orbs in my daughter's bedroom. Perhaps she can see them too, which explains why she may be up for three hours in the middle of the night.

Angels are a way of life. I cannot remember a time where they were not there to assist me in hardship or in joyful times. The angels have shown themselves as shapes of wings in the clouds, feathers at my door step, knocks on my bedroom window, orbs in our photos and most beautifully, tapping me on my left shoulder. To embrace our angels and spirit guides is to embrace the joy of being alive. May your life be filled with magic and childlike wonder when you connect with your angels!

How to Talk to your Angels using Breath Work

The angels have taught me various techniques to contact them and stay focused during healing work or meditation.

Many angel authors have written similar techniques and one technique is not better or stronger than the other. The pool of knowledge where this information comes is accessible to all. Everybody is unique; therefore finding a technique that suits you is a matter of trial and error. When I am learning new ways of exploring the angelic realms, I would often question *why*. Some people love the specifics and I am one of those.

The angels have taught me that breath work is a major key to be open to communication with angels and other spirit beings. In breath we absorb oxygen, and oxygen holds pure energy to clean away stale emotions, feelings and nervousness. There are many eastern cultures that know about the importance of breath work. We in the west are learning.

Throughout my story I have talked about breath in opening channels for communication with angels, in calming the body with Yoga and in hypno-birthing as a form of pain relief. The angels always talk about the importance of exercise, as the more oxygen we breathe in, the more we are open to angelic communication.

Breath Work

I like simple methods to get in touch with our spirit friends and I always find this one helpful.

- Have soft meditation music playing, candles and incense burning.

- Sit on a comfortable chair so you feel warm and cozy.

- Close your eyes and mentally say a short protection prayer such as, "I invoke God's grace which fills me with light. Light dissolves all darkness." Just by calling on God's light we are automatically working with the higher and more peaceful realms.

- Take a deep slow breath until you can't inhale any longer and then deeply exhale.

- Do this again another 2 times.

- Relax; you are now ready to hear the angels.

How to Hear or See the Angels

Many people see, hear or feel the angels in different formats. By preparing yourself with clean oxygen in your body, you would soon learn the technique most suitable for you. Perhaps you feel drawn to paint, draw, or you start seeing movie pictures in your mind's eye. You may hear words or get ideas. There is no right or wrong way.

Yoga Breath

The first time I went to a Hatha yoga class was at the angels' prompting. Yoga stretches the body to increase flexibility, and exercises internal organs and glands.

Yoga breath is very beneficial to go into a deep meditation, or for mild anxiety.

- Inhale air through the nose and bring the air down into your diaphragm so that it expands, bringing the abdomen slightly out.

- Exhale by expelling the air first from your abdomen and then from the upper lungs.

It is best to learn yoga from a yoga teacher as they can show you in great detail the correct breathing technique.

HypnoBirthing®

HypnoBirthing® is a natural childbirth technique, which teaches you that when there is no fear and tension, severe pain does not have to be part of labor. The method is a deep relaxation and self-hypnosis technique which eliminates the fear-tension-pain syndrome. Dr. Grantly Dick-Read, discovered that when laboring mothers were free of fear, their bodies relaxed; the muscles of their cervix relaxed and that permitted an easier natural birth. The internet is the best place to find your local HypnoBirthing® practitioner.

May the light of angels shine in your life always and may their guiding nudges propel you to a life of happiness and joy!

~

Bibliography
Bocelli, Andrea. *Romanza*. Philips, 1997.
Matthews, Simone. M. *Essence of Angels, Practitioner Course Manual*. Universal Life Tools, 2008.
Mongan, M.F. *HypnoBirthing-The Mongan Method*. Health Communication, Inc., 2005.
Virtue, Doreen. *Archangel Oracle Cards*. Hay house, 2004.

COBIE ANDREWS
Yateley, Hampshire, UK

COBIE ANDREWS QUALIFIED as an Angel Therapy Practitioner ® in 2008. She teaches workshops and offers private consultations to individual clients. She is a Principal of Angelic School Of Light©, which offers teaching to students who wish to become an Angelic Lightworker©. Cobie is also a trained Usui Reiki Master Teacher. In 2009 she published her first book entitled *I Believe.*

Cobie lives in a small town tucked away in the heart of Hampshire, with her husband Neil, three teenage sons Kylan, Terran, Devan and dog child Rufus. As a qualified Family Learning Tutor she teaches families and vulnerable young people who have been excluded from mainstream schools. Her specialist area is working with Indigos, supporting them with daily guidance.

Whether you would like to indulge yourself in angel energy relaxation, require guidance, or would like to find out more about becoming an Angelic Lightworker©, you'd be most welcome to visit her website www.healing senses.co.uk

It's Okay to be Different

COBIE ANDREWS

Indigo, crystal or rainbow children . . .
these terms refer to very sensitive, intuitive beings
of light and love, each with their own life purpose.

I watched the African sun lazily sink into the horizon from the comfort of my godparents' lounge, feeling the soft shag carpeting beneath my body. As I lay at my godfather's feet, I marveled at how simple, yet how complicated, life was. I knew that I was nine 'earth years' old, but I felt so much older. I knew I was surrounded by family who loved me, but I felt so alone. I had so many questions, but the answers to those questions seemed unreal. Tears of frustration rolled down my cheeks as I looked up at my godfather. I cleared my throat, working up the courage to ask him what I knew were the really difficult questions.

"Why was I born?" My young voice cut through the silence of the evening, making my godfather lay his newspaper across his lap and contemplate me. His face was kind as he looked at me and realized I was serious. His reply was simple. "You were born because God wants you here." I wasn't satisfied. *That's common knowledge,* I thought. So I tried again. "Yes, I know He wants me here. But why? What am I here for?"

My godfather exhaled a long breath as though he was buying time to think of a reply. He was used to my inquisitive nature, and it wasn't in *his* nature to back down from a challenge. "Well, Cobie, my dear, it seems to me that this is *exactly why* you are here on Earth," he said wisely. "You're here so that you may find your purpose in life."

Now *this* was an answer I had not considered! I was intrigued. A million ideas spun in my mind. I wanted to discuss them all with my godfather at length. But he had already picked up his paper again and was now reviewing the latest cricket scores and I didn't want to cause a fuss. I rolled over onto my stomach, stroking the shag carpeting, pretending to be a simple nine-year-old human who felt content with his reply. In truth, a door to a whole new universe of possibilities had been opened to me, and I could hardly wait to explore them. My journey had started.

That night, I silently prayed to God, "Just tell me, please! Just tell me what I am here to do!" Even though I was only nine, I was filled with an inexplicable sense of power and purpose and drive that, at times, almost felt overwhelming. I felt like the clock was ticking. I was running out of time! I was already behind!

Needless to say, I was an odd child. My oddness was compounded by the fact that I was living in a foreign country, Germany, while my father worked at the South African embassy. I had a tough enough time adjusting to my native culture and language, let alone dealing with a foreign one! I was also an incredibly sensitive child. I had more than 30 dolls stuffed in my room. I'd rescued most of them from the curb, dolls that others had wanted to throw away. I couldn't bear feeling their sadness, so I would 'adopt' them. Mother had her hands full, as my room was overflowing.

While I was having that conversation with God, I also mentioned to Him that I needed some friends. I didn't fit in. I didn't understand the ways of the people around me. "I hate feeling lost," I told God that night. "I hate not knowing what to do, not knowing how to fit in." I felt especially bad about causing my mother untold grief because I couldn't conform to the expectations of those around me. With guilt, I remembered the sadness in my mother's eyes as my first grade teacher confronted her after class.

"Cobie is the most stubborn child I have ever had to teach!" the frustrated teacher fumed. "The first in the history of the school to tear up her school books, saying over and over again that she was put in this school by accident, saying she was meant to be in University!" Even after that unpleasant meeting, my beloved mother didn't punish me or even blame me for my behavior. Instead, she guided me and coaxed me gently into understanding this world. In many ways, Mom was the answer to my prayers, over and over again.

A short time later, God did send the help that I prayed for, although I never could have imagined the path that it would lead me on. It was my first encounter with the angels. Mom and I had just returned to Germany after our visit with my godparents. I was playing with my dolls in my bedroom, surrounded by an orphanage of faces. Suddenly I was filled with warmth, and a strange, fuzzy feeling that I had never experienced before. It felt like all of the loving hugs I'd ever experienced in my lifetime, all at once. Even weirder, I felt like I was no longer alone in the room. I looked up, yet saw nothing.

That's odd, I thought, continuing to play. I always talked continually whilst playing, a kind of stream-of-consciousness monologue. But now, my monologue felt different, somehow. It felt like a *dialogue*, as though someone was talking back. Not minding the invisible company, I babbled away for hours until the fuzzy feeling dissipated. Over the next few days, the fuzzy feeling came over and over again, and stayed for longer periods of time. Finally, I became aware that the fuzzy feeling was constant. I felt a presence that never left my side. In fact, whenever I was in bed at night, the fuzzy feeling would increase exponentially.

Thanks to the fuzzy feeling, school was becoming almost bearable. I felt gently nudged, guided toward certain behaviors and steered away from others. Suddenly my school subjects began to make sense; Math, English, Reading and Art – it was as though a translator was suddenly speaking my language, helping me understand these formerly complicated subjects. I still didn't have many friends, but somehow it didn't matter anymore.

One evening my mother and father announced that they had news for us. My sisters and I gathered around quickly, excited to hear good news. My father spoke slowly. "The embassy has asked me to stay on here in Germany for another three years," he said as my mother stood beside him, a brave smile on her face. "I've accepted the offer." Father told us that the embassy was moving us to a new home in a few weeks. It would be much bigger and have more space for us all. He was right – our new home was huge. My sisters had their bedrooms on the third floor. My bedroom was on its own on the second floor, and my parents were downstairs from me.

"Will you be afraid to sleep in your room, all by yourself?" my mother asked, concerned. My reply was quick – perhaps too quick. "Oh, I'm not alone!" I chirped happily, exploring my space. My parents followed me. "What do you mean?" my father asked. This is when it occurred to me that my parents may not understand my fuzzy feeling, my newfound feeling of continual companionship. My mind raced. I remembered a movie that I'd seen on TV about a man who had what everyone *thought* was an imaginary friend." I have a rabbit!" I blurted out. "He's six feet, three-and-a-half inches tall, and his name is Harvey!" My parents' eyes met, and they had puzzled looks on their faces. Then they kind of shrugged at each other and let me be.

That night, I asked my fuzzy feeling if I could call him Harvey. The fuzzy feeling never said no, so I took the silence to mean yes. The next day, I bravely introduced Harvey to my sisters. I also introduced him properly to my parents. I have an awesome family – whether they purely indulged me or believed me, I still don't know to this day. It didn't matter. The introductions were made; Harvey became an accepted member of the family, and I was happy.

Shortly after we moved into the new house, my parents called me downstairs to the cellar. Not knowing what to expect, I was a bit hesitant at first. The cellar was huge, with three different rooms. One was the laundry room, which I loved. It smelt like roses and was always warm. The second room was long and spacious, and filled with mattresses on the floor. This is where my sisters and I often played gymnastics. My folks guided me to the third room, the storeroom where we kept excess furniture and boxes from the move. The door was closed, and I was puzzled. I opened the door. Inside was the most beautiful room I'd ever seen. It was set up like a little house. There were real lounge chairs with a coffee table, a cooker to the side, a lamp, and plenty of space for my dolls. My parents looked so pleased as I explored my new home for my dolls. It never occurred to me that all the furniture was faded and second hand; to me, it was totally awesome!

With Harvey by my side, I soon gathered all my dolls, cribs, cots, their clothes, nappies, bottles, and more. We were giggling and chatting away, thrilled with our new venture. One by one, my dolls each found their special place, and soon it was all complete. After a long day, I stood back and marveled at the glorious view of everyone feeling loved and protected. The energy was buzzing with joy. To some, it might have been an overkill of a dolls' house. To me, however, it was an orphanage of love. Harvey and I had our hands full, with 32 mouths to feed, nappies to change, and not to mention all the washing. Thank goodness we were next to the laundry! Looking back today, I realize that at that moment, I finally became content with who I am.

Despite Harvey's help and company, I still struggled at school, struggling with even the simplest of things. My fifth grade teacher was originally from Hawaii, and had taken it upon herself to teach us how to hula dance. I really wanted to be able to dance the hula, but I was hopelessly uncoordinated. Plus, my mind wandered endlessly, enticed by the rhythmic music. My frustrated teacher made it her own personal mission to make me learn to hula, sequestering me during lunch breaks, coaching me to bend my knees at precise angles, urging me to swing my hips at a varied pace whilst taking slip-sliding steps and making wave motions with my arms. It was the ultimate case of information overload to my young mind! But I was desperate to impress and please my teacher. Most important, I was determined to conquer this challenge! I endured the training with willful pride. As I lay in bed at night, strains of the music still lingered in my mind. My thoughts drifted lazily to a moment lost in time, to a culture where everything was natural and not forced. Would I ever be able to do the hula?

> **Angelic Support**
>
> *Your angels want you to know that you are never alone.*
>
> *Angels are forever watching over you, offering you loving guidance and support. They will intervene on your behalf if ever you are in danger. The moment you ask, angelic comfort, protection and support are instantly available to you!*

Harvey! I called to my friend silently. He was there in a moment, as though he already knew the favor I sought. I sensed the rhythm of the music filling my body and gently stretched out my arms, making the waving motions my teacher had tried so hard to help me understand. To my surprise, it was as though my arms had left my body as they gently started making motions of waves to absolute perfection. Furthermore, my arms were surrounded by the most beautiful colors of the rainbow, buzzing with energy of true delight.

As I lay there watching the beautiful arms, completely overtaken by magical pleasure, I noticed a shadow on the wall. I gasped with surprise and nearly swallowed my tongue. There on my bedroom wall, in colours swirling with delight was the outline of what I can only describe as a flowing, rainbow swirl. The shadow was gently guiding my arms into the wave motions, playfully, lightly, up and down, delicate movements of pleasure. I mustered up the courage and with a dry throat croaked, "Harvey, is that you? Is that really you?" The shadow of colours seemed to nod, and in my heart I felt it was him. Layers of initial fear drifted away as the realization of Harvey surrounded my existence.

In the vast world of my childish imagination, I had many commitments and obligations. As I sat on the swing in my backyard, I would be interviewed on various life-changing topics in my mind. As gravity pulled me forward, I would elevate audiences to higher levels of understanding with my wisdom. As force swung me back, I would create world peace and harmony through my wit and ingenuity, whooshing through the air, four feet off the ground. I could go on like this for hours. If anyone asked where I was, Mom would say, "She's far away, swinging, solving the problems of the world. Best we let her be for a little while yet. She'll come in when she's ready."

It was also during these sessions of swinging that I seemed to learn much about the world. Harvey would explain to me in detail why people were behaving as they were. He'd show me options of how to deal with situations, as well as their outcomes. From these conversations with Harvey, I would go on in my imagination to teach others about my experiences.

"Everything will be okay," I imagined myself telling audiences. "It's okay to be different! We actually all are different! Some just don't realize it. They shrug this off in a rush to conform to what they see as the norm and the expected." In my mind's eye, I could see the members of my imaginary audience nod and smile, their consciousnesses illuminated by my words. Harvey's beautiful colors would surround me constantly, indicating his presence, assuring me of his love. In my imagination, and in real life, my world was perfect in many ways.

Time slipped past in a blur as I grew and developed into a teenager. I knew that Harvey was still with me, yet we connected infrequently. When I intentionally made contact with Harvey, our interactions were subdued. I felt okay without him constantly by my side, but only because I knew he was never far away. In hindsight, I realize that Harvey had become part of who I was at my core. He was living through me, through my thoughts and actions, radiating through my very being. I had become so accustomed to Harvey, I rarely noticed him as a separate being anymore. Strangely, at this point I had still not questioned Harvey's origins. My relationship with him was one of pure, naive acceptance. It just felt right.

Years passed. I became an adult, a wife, and a mother to three beautiful, very different, endearing boys. With each passing year, the memories and aspirations of my childhood seemed to fade, and Harvey seemed but a distant, pleasant dream.

When my mother passed away, I was engulfed with grief. She was the cornerstone of my life. The foundation of my existence had crumbled. I remained inconsolable and felt I had no one to turn to. My doctor prescribed medication to help me cope. Unfortunately I saw this as a solution to *avoid* coping. After a long time, someone referred me to a wonderful psychologist who also practiced homeopathy and hypnotherapy, a profoundly spiritual man.

As I sat in his office one afternoon, I found myself uttering familiar words.

"Why am I here on Earth?" He looked at me for a long while, and for a moment I thought he was going to say, "Have you learnt nothing woman? For nearly a year, I have seen you once a week, and you still dare to ask such a shallow question!"

Of course, he didn't say that. Instead, he took a piece of paper and scribbled something down. *There,* I thought, *finally, someone with answers!* Handing me the paper, he said, "I thought you'd never ask. Contact this lady. You're ready." Eagerly I phoned the number as soon as I got home, giving her my details and making an appointment. My mood had lightened, and I felt like I had won some sort of bonanza prize. I couldn't imagine what this woman would tell me, but I knew something amazing was about to happen.

When we finally met my new mentor, it felt like we'd only spent a few minutes together – in fact, we spoke for several hours. We talked about the events of my life, and how I had come to where I was. Everything felt right; I felt understood and supported. Whilst we were talking, the beautiful familiar buzzing feeling of Harvey returned. It was as though he had waited for many years to physically reappear, waiting for just the right moment in which I would accept his true being. My mentor looked to my side as I proceeded to tell her about my invisible friend. "He's six feet, three-and-a-half inches tall, and his name is Harvey," I told her, just as I'd told my family so many years ago.

"I can see! He's a beautiful angel, indeed," she replied, nodding. I was puzzled for a moment, even questioning her sanity. *Is she having a laugh?* I thought, almost immediately regretting that I shared Harvey with her at all. She must have seen the confusion written on my face. "Harvey is your guardian angel," she explained gently.

In that moment, all of the seemingly fractured puzzle pieces of my life seemed to snap into place, and things started to make sense. My life came into focus. I finally understood the world.

In 2008 I had the privilege to travel to Hawaii, where a new chapter in my life began. Upon arrival in Kona, I laid crystals in a grid and paid tribute to my fifth grade teacher who inadvertently had played a very important role in my life. I trained as an Angel Therapy Practitioner and returned later that year to complete my advanced training.

Why am I here on Earth? I am a Lightworker, and I am here to guide, support, and share with all humankind, the marvels of life.

Understanding Yourself

My experiences both personally and professionally have all contributed to create an understanding of just how difficult it can be for young and old alike to fit into this world. Everyone seems to strive to be a part of the *norm*. My dear friends, let the truth be told today: The *norm* is you – it is what makes you feel happy and comfortable, and it is what allows you to flourish at your own pace.

You have probably heard that our young ones born from the early 1990s are being referred to as either indigo, crystal or rainbow children. Those born prior to 1990 are referred to as scouts. These terms are signposts used in order for us to understand that they resonate with a particular energy that has unique qualities. In a nutshell, these terms refer to people who are very sensitive, intuitive beings of light and love, each with their own life purpose. They are passionate, creative, and have much to offer our world. The indigos are here to bring about change, a difficult task! The crystals bring with them the insight and support to show us the way to a brighter future. Our dear rainbows have come with harmony to bring ultimate peace and acceptance.

If any part of my story reminds you of a young one in your life, even in the slightest way, I urge you to support and guide them with extra gentle care. My mother truly had her hands full with me as a child. I'd take the bathroom mirror outside and hold it shining up to the clouds so that I could look down into it and pretend I was walking on clouds, or wake everyone up in the middle of the night to show them the beautiful night sky through the ceiling, as I could see it. I was never scolded; my family embraced me, sheltered me and above all accepted me for who I was. I ask that you will do the same.

There will always be a memory of 'Home' and although we all share the same memories, it is our sensitive young ones who remember it more vividly. That is, if they are permitted to. So often I work with parents whose children have recently been diagnosed with ADD, ADHD or ASD. They cry long tears of despair in my office, begging for support, ridden with overwhelming feelings of guilt. I ask those parents: "How has your child changed since the diagnosis?" They stare at me with a blank look, amazed. Their answers are always the same." Well, they don't know that they've been diagnosed. They're the same as always." I have found the best way forward is to allow the young ones to simply be themselves. There is a wealth of knowledge and support available in this world. Find that which resonates with you and apply it with love and inner guidance.

To those who have struggled to be accepted in this world because of who you are, I offer the following: When you decide to take a trip to a new destination, let's say London, how do you go about planning your trip? You do research, plan your route and prepare for the journey. Once you are en route, you follow all the indicated signs. However, once you have reached your destination, do you still look for the London signs, or do you simply relax and enjoy your new destination? The answer is clear: you enjoy where you are in the moment! This is my wish for you. Come to know yourself, and then simply follow the signs of who you are. Become content with this, and embrace yourself. Believe that beautiful angels will follow and support you all the way and help you see the marvels of yourself. It's okay to be different, because we are all unique.

Archangel Michael, Archangel Metatron, and Archangel Raphael are particularly helpful in this regard. Archangel Michael will support you with feeling safe and guide you along your journey with protection and humor. Archangel Metatron is an awesome interpreter to those who have the need to comprehend. He is brilliant in helping us analyze and understand, especially in areas such as math and science. Archangel Raphael will shower you with love, giving you energy and revitalizing you with unconditional love. He also allows you to accept yourself and others with love, and helps you to release all guilt or low self esteem.

By using daily positive affirmations, calling upon the archangels for support and guidance, you will be able to maintain a level of compassion for yourself and life in general.

Positive Affirmations and Asking the Angels for Support

Archangel Metatron:

"Dear Archangel Metatron, I call upon your skills of interpretation in understanding myself and the beautiful world around me. Thank you for supporting me to clearly understand this situation (state your own situation), so that I may have compassion for myself and others. This situation is now resolved and understood. I feel supported. I understand myself and others. I am able to comprehend with ease. And so it is."

Angel Chamuel:

"Loving Chamuel, I call upon you to show me and (child's name) the way forward with (name the situation), with unconditional love, understanding and total acceptance. Please shower us both in your golden light, allowing us to move forward with grace and compassion. Thank you for shielding (young one's name) from harsh energies, protecting and guiding them with your gentle embrace. Thank you.

Archangel Raphael:

"Dear Archangel Raphael, I call upon your energy of love and rejuvenation. Thank you for guiding me through each day with renewed inspiration and love for myself and others, allowing me to become one with unconditional self love. I see myself (explain in your own words), and request your help to enable me to see myself through your eyes, clearing away all judgments against myself and releasing guilt, anger and hurt from previous experiences in all directions of time. I am loved. I am worthy. I am unique. And so it is."

Archangel Michael:

"Dear Archangel Michael, I call upon you now for support and wisdom. I am grateful that I am able to see myself clearly, allowing my journey to take its planned course with ease and love. Please help me to embrace the humor of life to the full.

Everything in my life is in complete order, just the way it should be. All is well in my life. I am protected. I am happy. And so it is."

∽

DEBBIE KOSABEK
Regina, Saskatchewan, Canada

DEBBIE KOSABEK IS an Angel Therapy Practitioner® and medium, certified by Dr. Doreen Virtue Ph D. Debbie has participated in Advanced Angel Therapy training and is Certified in Past Life Healing by Dr. Doreen Virtue, PhD. She is currently completing a degree in Metaphysics and is a Reiki Practitioner Level II. She is an intuitive and a channel for the angelic realms.

Debbie lives in Regina, Saskatchewan, Canada and assists clients through readings, consultations and workshops. Her mission is to assist people to find the love in life by moving past their blocks and fears so they can discover their true purpose, naturally connecting with the love in their life's work. Debbie is a spiritual speaker and author of *Auntie, How do you Talk to God?* She has also been published in *WHOLifE Journal*, writing various articles about her spiritual work with the angels.

She has produced two meditation CDs, Angelic *Meditations* and *Adventures of the Soul*.

Visit Debbie's website at www.angelliteandlove.com

The Miracle of Three

DEBBIE KOSABEK

I now realize my nephews belong to a new generation
of children called the Crystal children.
These children are highly sensitive, forgiving, and easygoing.

When I was thirty-two years old, my second marriage ended. I was finan-cially and emotionally devastated. And I was angry! I had no idea who I was anymore. How could I survive in a world where no one could be trusted, no one really loved, and nothing ever lasted? As time passed, I began to regain my position of security – financially, anyway, thanks to my loving and supportive family. Emotionally, I was struggling; the only way to cope was to bury myself in my work.

I worked in an acute-care hospital as a registered nurse, caring for those who had cancer, or those who were recovering from illness or surgery. I loved this work, pouring my heart and soul into supporting these people during their hospital stay and sometimes supporting them through their last minutes on this earth. Here I could care for people in a way that was personally safe. Patients and their fami-lies, for the most part, were grateful for the kindness and caring provided, and their gratitude filled a very real need in my heart. Outside of work, however, I felt nothing but a void that made my heart ache. I knew something had to change, but what? And how? I wept each and every night. As I lay in my empty bed, I prayed for help, for someone to love and for someone to love me. I prayed for someone tall, dark and handsome to come into my life. Then an ugly fear would fill my head – maybe I wasn't loveable! The very thought would make the tears flow again.

In the midst of all this turmoil, a miracle occurred. My brother and his wife got pregnant. I was going to be an auntie! I waited for the moment when my sister-in-law's labor began, not sure of what to expect, and indeed, having not a clue what I would feel. Finally, my brother called with happy news. It was eight o'clock in the evening; Marie was in labor, they were heading to the hospital, and he would call as soon as the baby came.

The night passed without a call. When morning came, I considered calling in sick but thought better of it, given the staffing conditions in my workplace. I arrived at work and waited, but no call came. The morning passed with my mind constantly straying to my sister-in-law. I could barely concentrate and found myself standing and staring at the medication book instead of doing my work. I felt an uncomfortable tightness in my belly and throat; I tried to rationalize the discomfort away, thinking it was just excitement.

By now my sister-in-law had been in labor 24 hours – too long. It was two in the afternoon and a hush had fallen over the ward. I was beside myself and decided to call the birthing unit one more time. If there was still no news, I would ask for permission to leave and go to them.

The phone seemed to ring a hundred times before someone answered. Finally, my brother came on the line. "We have a baby boy," he said. "He was just born, and he was not breathing when he came out, but he is fine now and has gone to the baby intensive care." I was stunned, at a loss for words. Tears filled my eyes and my throat tightened even further at the thought of what might have been. All I could say to him was, "Thank God! What took so long?"

He didn't have an answer. I spoke with Marie, promising to go to the hospital as soon as I got off work. Then I went to the washroom and cried. Great tears rolled down my cheeks, washing away the fear that had gripped me throughout the day. When I finally left the washroom, I gave my colleagues the good news: I was an auntie to a beautiful baby boy!

I was so grateful that he was fine, but the lingering fear of 'what could have been' affected me deeply. There was something about this entire experience that was ethereal. I had so much love for this little guy; I had loved him long before this day. We were connected in spirit and in our hearts in some special way that I could not explain. In that moment, I thanked God for keeping him safe and bringing him to us, whole and healthy. I was filled with gratitude for this gift of life.

As soon as I was done with my shift, I went to see the new family. Technically, only parents and grandparents were allowed to visit newborns in the ICU, but there was no stopping me! I gowned up and went in to gaze upon my nephew Curtis for the very first time. He was beautiful, pink, and peaceful. Everything about him was perfect.

I returned the next day, happy to find him in his mother's room. As I held him for the first time, an unfamiliar feeling washed over me. I gazed into his face and felt a love so great, it was as if my chest was about to explode. So much emotion! Right then and there, I silently pledged to love and protect him, forever and ever.

As I continued to gaze at him, I said, "Yes, I love you, too!"

I kissed him for the first time on his little forehead. My sister-in-law gave me a strange look and said, "What are you doing?"

"Well," I replied, "Curtis just told me he loves me, and we're talking!"

She shook her head – perhaps she thought I was acting a little crazy. Then she simply shrugged her shoulders and gave a wee smile. As I continued to cradle my tiny nephew, I came to know what loving from the deepest part of my soul was all about. I realized there was so much more to life. This wondrous gift, this sweet child's presence in my life, was a miracle. That day my heart began to open and I began to heal.

I spent many hours with my beautiful nephew, caring for him, playing with him and adoring him. Curtis was a delightful baby, full of smiles and love. He had a smile that could melt your heart, and as he got older, he was always trying to make people laugh. It was like he was trying to tell us, "Lighten up! Laughter is good for the soul!"

Four years after Curtis' birth, I was blessed once more with another little nephew. Corey was born on a cold and stormy February day. Once again, I felt the outpouring of love and joy as I cradled this new little life in my arms.

When I wasn't busy with my nephews, I spent my time in solitude, finding a certain comfort in the silence. For two years, I basically dissected every aspect of my life with the skill of a well-trained surgeon. My romantic misadventures had made me a cynical woman, filled with pain and anger. I realized I had allowed my desire to be in a relationship to alter the way I was as a person. I lost myself in those relationships. I did things and said things that I wasn't proud of. I also lost my boundaries. I thought about life in general – what it was all about, where I was in my personal journey, and how I had become the person I was. What kind of person would I be proud to become? I had a sense that I was at a crossroads. I could choose where my journey would take me next. It was time to discover 'me' again, I decided. Only then would I be capable of accepting and recognizing real love. One thing I knew for certain: I was capable of real love – I felt it for my sweet nephews.

> **Dreams**
>
> *Your dreams hold important messages for you from your angels.*
>
> *Keep a Dream Journal and write whatever you recall of your dreams upon waking. Your dreams contain instruction from your higher self and messages from your angels. Pay attention to their loving advice.*

My third nephew, Kirk, arrived just one year after Corey. It had been a tumultuous pregnancy for his mother. When she told me about the pregnancy, I instantly said, "There is a special reason why this baby is coming into our world." At that time, I felt an overwhelming love for this unborn child and a need to protect him, always.

Kirky arrived, beautiful to behold. One afternoon when he was four months old, we were all in the back yard, lush and green, with the sun shining down upon us. My brother motioned for me to look at the baby he held in his arms. He whispered, "I think someone really loves you!" My brother's usually well-controlled countenance had softened, and his eyes filled with tears as if he, too, could sense the love exchange. My nephew was staring at me – it was as if he looked into my very soul, and his gaze would not shift. These were the eyes of innocence. They were love, pure and whole, these eyes gazing back at me. Like the angels, this pure love saw me beyond all the layers of fear, control and worry of an adult life. These eyes saw the beautiful child within me – the pure love that still exists. I was receiving a healing through my baby nephew, through his pure and loving gaze and the exchange of pure love energy.

As we connected, I became aware that my heart was still waiting to open fully, and that I longed to share the miracle of me with all of humanity. I longed to let go of the fear that gripped me when I thought about opening my heart completely, though it was fully and completely open to the innocent love of my nephews.

When I arrived home that evening, I felt warm and fuzzy all over. I realized that loving my nephews and others in my life was the most important thing in the universe. I also realized that spending time with those I loved was the most amazing gift I could possibly give them, the most valuable gift I could give them.

Suddenly, a passage from a book I had read months before came to me.

> *The spirit transforms, grows, and matures by accepting truths,*
> *by facing troubles, by overcoming temptations,*
> *and by learning how to love and forgive.*
> *What happens outwardly in life is not as important*
> *as what happens within; sometimes,*
> *change and growth take a lifetime.*

–RICK WARREN, *The Purpose Driven Life*

In that moment, I realized the past several years had been a journey of spiritual transformation and awakening to love in its purest sense. I realized I was not only capable of *giving* great love, but worthy of *receiving* great love, as well. I knew now that opening my heart to give and receive great love would open the pathways to explore all of life's possibilities through the eyes of love.

I began to realize my interest in angels was *something*! A really big something! The angels had been working with me throughout my life, connecting in so many different ways. The beautiful trees and flowerbeds in my garden are graced with statues of angels and fairies, as are the rooms of my home. My very first Seraphim angel was a Christmas gift from Curtis, when he was just three months of age. The collection has since grown to fill my china cabinet. When my brother asks his sons, "What would Auntie like for Christmas?" Curtis always answers, "I know what you want, Auntie! You want angels."

These boys are my own angel ambassadors and the answer to my prayers for someone to love. Indeed, fifteen years later Curtis is tall, dark and handsome, living proof that our prayers are answered but not always in the way we think they should be! They have an innate spiritual connection to the angels, and I am committed to supporting them in maintaining that connection. The miracle of my nephews continued, as my life was filled with joy and blessed with love in every moment shared with them. As long as I can remember they have been very comfortable with angels.

I now realize my nephews belong to a new generation of children called the Crystal children. These children are highly sensitive, forgiving, and easygoing. The newborn Crystal child's eyes are described as magnetic. They have large eyes with an intense stare. Crystal children may start talking later in childhood, as they tend to connect on a telepathic level quite naturally and find no need to talk. Curtis was indeed a late bloomer when it came to verbal communication. My dear sister in law was distraught over this – yet now he is a straight 'A' student, oh yes, but still the strong, silent type.

Crystal children are sweet and loving, and very connected to nature and animals. All three boys love the outdoors and are in fact quite miserable if cooped up inside for too long! They are cuddly, caring, and display an unprecedented level of kindness and sensitivity. My youngest nephew, Kirky, gives everyone hugs, long hugs including kisses and wide eyed loving looks. These children are said to give healing doses of love everywhere they go.

They are also fearless explorers and climbers. I recall his sweet voice one afternoon as he stood before me, his small hand clasped into a fist and raised above his head in a victory display saying " I am fearless, Auntie!!!" The Crystal children have an authoritative air about them, as if they're wise adults in little bodies. They cannot tolerate lies or deceitfulness. The middle child, Corey, constantly corrects us, his parents included, with little discrepancies in stories, speaking so directly – "Dad that just isn't true!" He constantly watches the speedometer when we are driving, reminding me if I am going too fast.

As my three nephews grew, it was a delight to observe each one developing his own unique personality and talents. Often I notice how much Curtis and Kirk resemble each other. My brother often comments on how "They are like two peas in a pod." They stick together and are always hugging and kissing each other. When one gets into trouble, the other is not far behind to help him out of it or into it!! I have learned that a Crystal child may be sent into a home to be a support to another child. This is often the case if the parents are not open spiritually. It is also common that these children have a grandparent or other close relative that is meant to be their spiritual guardian.

My nephews often spend time with me. On one of these occasions it was the beginning of summer and we spent a fabulous week together. We played, talked, hugged, and went to all our favorite places to eat. They continued to show interest in my angel oracle card decks that I have scattered throughout the house, and they asked questions endlessly.

"How do you know I have my own guardian angels?" Corey asked.

Curtis added, "Can we ask the angels questions? Can we try your cards out?"

The angels weren't the kids' only focus, though. The boys couldn't keep their hands off my crystals, either. All three boys huddled around my living room coffee table, looking at the large amethyst crystal that I'd recently purchased. The youngest picked it up and studied it thoroughly. Later that morning they settled into their favorite spots in the kitchen for snack time and Kirky asked me, "Auntie, how do you talk to God and what about the angels?"

I was ill prepared to reply to his question at that moment, although it continued to haunt me over the following days and months. I would wake up thinking about this latest question and an answer began to develop. Morning after morning, the answer became crystal clear along with the feeling to write the information in book format. Finally I gave in. I jumped out of bed and typed it all into a document. I realize now this whole experience was divinely guided and the angels wanted this important message shared with everyone. I must say, being an auntie has meant far more than I ever thought it would, as the complex questions just keep on coming. Truthfully, I am honored that I hold the boys' trust, as they ask anything without being judged or criticized. It was no coincidence, these questions popping up, just as it was no coincidence that these boys came into my life.

A year-and-a-half later it came to be, a little book in answer to my nephew's question, *Auntie, How Do You Talk to God?* The book contained a message about the oneness of life, nature, animals, humans, God, and the angels – a message that love is in all of life.

The book was a message of affirmation that God and the angels hear our requests and answer them. My intent was to create a book that children in first and second grades could read and understand. The more I thought about it, the more I became aware that we were painting a picture of Spirit, based on the ideology that God is in all things. The more I thought about it, the more I realized the message contained in this book was not only for children, it was for adults as well.

And then the angels gave me this very special message: "You never know who this book is meant for or in whose hands it will land. What you will know is this message of love will help to change the way we view the world and the way we live in it day to day."

The greatest joy of all was watching Kirky read this book as I sat patiently beside him.

Now eight years old, he read the text with ease. I noticed how he would pause and reflect on a particular section that he had just read. I noticed his smiles and even a giggle at his favorite part about "the ants," which speaks to all things being important, no matter how big or small.

The angels work in magical and mystical ways. Together, my beautiful nephews and the angels have given me inspiration to do things in this life I never dreamed of. My children's book has forced discussions with family and friends about my work with the angels. Now, I am in a position to support and care for my family spiritually, and to encourage my nephews' own innate spiritual gifts and their life path.

It is with loving gratitude that I thank the angels and God for all the miracles in my life, especially the three small miracles sent to help heal my life from anger, pain and betrayal, the three small miracles sent to open my heart to love and to the light of God and the angels, the three small miracles who helped me believe in 'me.' They have helped me find the courage to open my heart to love and prepare to share my life with my Soulmate. They have given me the courage to see through the eyes of love in all areas of my life. They have given me the courage to continue to grow along my spiritual path and share the light that dwells within me with all who seek it.

Angels and Creativity
When we speak of creativity, inevitably the word 'inspiration' arises. This word originates from the word 'spirit' and originally meant 'the breath of divinity.' Inspiration signifies that a leap of insight has cut across boundaries from the normal process of reasoning to the creative moment. In a spiritual context, creativity requires the abandonment of ego control and a willingness to receive the 'word of spirit/angels,' to tap into the great universal consciousness. And it also requires then that once the inspiration is received that we act upon it with faith and passion.

The angels are ever ready and willing to assist us with divine inspiration to move us along our path as Lightworkers, with the ultimate intention of bringing the world and all its inhabitants closer to a loving, peaceful existence. Our angels are in constant communication with us. However, we may not always be ready or willing to receive these communications. It is natural then, that our angels will connect with us when we are in states of consciousness where our ego has little or no control over our thoughts. The first of these natural states is our sleep time, the second during meditation.

When we sleep, our natural fears, barriers and conflicts disappear, replaced by a stillness of consciousness where our angels can freely communicate with us. Angel visitations, healings and inspirations received during dream time have been documented for eons in scripture – for example, Jacob's Ladder, the ladder to heaven, described in the Book of Genesis, which the biblical patriarch Jacob envisions during dream time.

To enhance this naturally powerful method of communicating with our angels, set the intention prior to drifting off to sleep using a simple affirmation such as: "Angels please come into my dreams tonight to bring me healing/creative inspiration / a solution to . . . . , and I affirm that I will remember clearly your messages when I awake in the morning." I have received many visits and inspirational messages from my angels during dreamtime. The entire script for my children's book *Auntie, How do you Talk to God* was received just at that time between sleep and wakening. I also received inspiration for the book's artwork, through very vivid and colorful dream visions.

I recommend journaling of these dreams for future reference. Unless we are very accomplished dream travelers, our dreams tend to fade and detail is lost to us forever. So journaling about dreams on waking is a highly effective practice. Dreams are the mysterious language of the night. These secret messages can foretell the future, reveal the past and warn you of danger. They can bring inspiration and creativity and assist in melting barriers in your life. Dreams serve as a doorway to communication with the higher realms.

Meditative practice creates much the same doorway during waking hours. All ancient peoples, cultures and civilizations used some form of meditation. Humans have longed for connection with spirit and somehow these ancient people knew that through silence, and looking inward, a doorway opens. Through this doorway we begin to connect with our higher consciousness, with spirit. Our energy bodies begin to resonate at a higher frequency, much closer to that of the angels and spirit. In truth we are bringing Heaven closer to us, so we naturally experience all the gifts that accompany this.

When we invite the angels into our meditation experiences through creative visualization, we are inviting these powerful loving and healing light beings into our life. Sit down with a pen and paper and write about your meditative experiences. Write down everything you saw, heard and felt during the meditation. This grounds the information and makes it real to you in this human existence, and also provides a record to reference into the future.

Over the next days and months you will notice an increase in your own dream activity. I invite you to embrace this experience as you have invited the angelic kingdom into your life – miracles are about to happen for you!

Bedtime Visualization to Enhance Dreaming
Close your eyes and take a few deep breaths and relax. On your next breath in, imagine you are standing outside on a beautiful moonlit night. You see the stars overhead and the beautiful full moon above. You notice a mist beginning to form; it swirls and dances and draws closer to you. Out of the mist steps a beautiful angel, dressed in silvery robes with long blonde hair and you instinctively know this is the Archangel Haniel – master of clairvoyance and intuition. You feel her loving energy as she comes to stand before you.

Archangel Haniel is holding a beautiful white velvet cloth that is glowing in white and silver light. As she gently reaches forward and begins to rub the spot between your two physical eyes, you feel a slight pressure and a warmth. Then you see debris flying outward, dark specks that have the appearance of pieces of coal. As Haniel continues to gently clean your third eye, you see geometric shapes floating before you. She asks you to breathe, to relax, as all is well and good. She asks you to silently affirm "I now remember my dreams. I invite the angels into my dreams to bring me healing messages tonight." You silently thank Archangel Haniel. Take another deep breath and drift off to sleep.

Awareness

Your angels honor your profound awareness as a deeply sensitive being.

You are extremely sensitive to your surroundings, so try to avoid harsh environments or potentially toxic situations. Use your acute awareness instead to connect with the cycles of the moon or to work with healing tools like crystals, herbs or essential oils.

BELINDA RIDLEY
Wagga Wagga, NSW, Australia

BELINDA RIDLEY is an Angel Intuitive™ with advanced training, certified by Doreen Virtue, PhD. She is also a trained Reiki Seichim Master teacher. Having completed her Diploma in Community Services of Welfare, Belinda now works with the elderly as a Diversional Therapist in Wagga Wagga. Belinda has also undertaken studies in Hot Stone Massage, Relaxation Massage and Seraphim Healing. She uses her combined skills and experience to conduct readings and healing work through her business Inner Connections.

Belinda loves traveling the world, having new adventures and learning about different cultures. She loves to express herself creatively through her artwork, writing, dancing, acting and singing. Another passion of Belinda's is the combination of dreams and crystals.

Belinda has the philosophy of lighting as many candles along the way in life as she can. She does this by spreading joy! She also believes that life is a sacred and wondrous learning journey and that embracing and sharing love is one of the most important keys to living a fulfilling life. Belinda is passionate about helping others to find their own inner strength, peace and wisdom.

You can contact Belinda at soulsister_63@hotmail.com

Angelic Dreams of Love and Guidance

BELINDA RIDLEY

Our deepest fear is not that we are inadequate.
Our deepest fear is that we are powerful beyond measure.
It is our light, not our darkness that most frightens us.

—MARIANNE WILLIAMSON

*A*ngels have been a large part of my life for many years now. Ever since I was a young girl I was strongly in tune and connected with my higher self and God. I attended church on a weekly basis with my grandparents and I remember feeling that God was always with me because he lived inside my heart. Even though I was a very spiritual young girl, at this stage I do not have a conscious memory of angels though I know for sure now that they have been with me along my entire journey, and will continue to be with me for all eternity.

I began to be greatly influenced by angelic information about ten years ago. My mother had begun researching and taking many metaphysical courses, and being a very passionate woman, she shared numerous things she had learnt whilst undertaking these courses. I remember her telling me that Archangel Michael was always with me to protect me and this made me feel very safe. Whenever I felt in any danger or if ever I felt slightly afraid, I would mentally say "Archangel Michael protect me," and I still use this now continuously.

I went through a very rough and deeply challenging period in my life at the end of 2002, as I battled some of my deepest and darkest fears. I felt extremely dependant on those around me to feel validated and loved and was terrified of being alone. I had just left my first serious relationship, only to go straight into another one. I didn't give myself any time to grieve, though grieving is exactly what I truly needed. I was letting go of someone who'd been a huge part of my life, someone I had allowed into my heart. This was the first partner to love me for me, and leaving this person was the most hurtful thing I had ever experienced. I couldn't believe how something like this could hurt so much.

I had harbored a lot of guilt in my life previously and had a belief that things were 'always my fault.' This way of thinking had an extremely cruel effect upon my well-being. So, leaving my first relationship was no exception. I blamed myself for all the pain I had caused my partner, telling myself I was unforgivable. I rejected my own pain and grief, telling myself that I didn't deserve to even feel pain since I had inflicted so much upon another human being. If ever I started to feel good for a short time, somehow my mind would come up with a way of telling me why I didn't deserve happiness. I would remember something I had done and then feel consumed by the shame at this proof (so I thought) of my being a terribly bad person.

I found it very difficult to forgive myself and move forward, so I tried to block the guilt and these memories out of my mind. But they were always there ready to bring me down, usually just as I was starting to feel good. At that stage in my life I was feeling incredibly lost, confused, low and out of control. I was ignoring what was in my heart because it scared me. I felt terribly alone and didn't know what to do. And that's when it happened . . .

Intention

Your intentions are what create your experiences in life.

Allow the angels to help you set new intentions as you visualize your life as successful, happy and peaceful. Replace any old life patterns or outworn beliefs with empowering, loving intentions to create the life of your dreams.

I had a dream but it wasn't just any old dream. Though I do believe that all dreams are special and unique in their own way, this dream was angelic and profound. I remember as clear as day that I was greeted by an angel. The angel appeared quite normal, but the energy of this being let me know he was in fact an angel. He looked at me with so much love, smiling a jolly and caring smile. I remember feeling elated, as if all my problems were miles away. The angel said that he had something to show me. When I followed the angel, this special being proceeded to show me the events in my life that were making me feel very guilty. However something was different. The angel was showing me the events from his point of view, saying "This is how we see it." I was able to see the events through the eyes of an angel for that brief and magical moment in time. Not one ounce of guilt, shame or judgment surfaced within me as I watched these events. I didn't label them as good or bad. I even felt a little happy and entertained by what I was seeing. It was amazing!

When we had come to the end of viewing these events I knew that I was in the presence of a truly magnificent being and I asked the angel, "What is the meaning of life?" With a cheeky, all-knowing smile upon his beautiful, angelic face he told me, "You will not remember." Nevertheless, he continued to tell me the meaning of life. I remember being utterly fascinated and flabbergasted, secretly trying to store it in my memory and then wake myself up so as to keep the meaning clearly in my mind. I awoke and sprung into an upright position, then quickly shook my friend awake to tell him "I found out what the meaning of life is!" With anticipation in his voice my friend asked, "What is it?" I tried to answer but what the angel had said with his all-knowing smile was true. "Ah!" I moaned with frustration. "The angel *told* me I wouldn't remember!" But I smiled to myself as I saw how incredibly humorous it was that I had tried to outwit an angel.

This magical, angelic dream was a huge beginning for me. It was the first time in my life that I had experienced what it felt like to not feel guilt inside of me, to not feel ashamed of who I was and of the decisions I had made throughout my life. I'm not saying that it all happened over night because it didn't, but at this extremely challenging time, where I felt like I was falling apart inside, my angels were there to guide me. I was given what I needed at the time to unblock my emotions and I began to move forward in my life. I was then able to face many fears, which I had been running from for years. Some turned out to be nothing, but I had been so afraid that I gave them more and more unnecessary energy. I had so many fears! I felt I wasn't a powerful or capable being. I didn't feel worthy of good things coming into my life.

I would run from myself and spend all of my time in the company of others so I wouldn't have to really be alone with myself. I was in a new relationship, which unfortunately brought disappointment after disappointment. I was too afraid to leave because this would mean that I would have to be alone . . . and that was my greatest fear. I was afraid that I wasn't capable of being alone and that I couldn't rely on myself to get through life's challenges on my own.

It was at this time that my mother and I began conducting angel nights on a weekly basis. This consisted of each person researching an angel of their choice and then we would come together once a week and share what we had learned. I was intuitively aware that each time I researched an angel, I seemed to draw that particular angel to me. Angel nights were a magical, healing, informative and wonderful experience, though if I am honest with myself, I still felt rather depressed, scared and unhappy with my life.

One night we had been listening as my mother shared her knowledge of Archangel Raziel. It was lovely. I was fairly uptight in those days so I remember this night very clearly. I had stayed at my friend's house that night after our angel gathering, where I awoke feeling energized, awake, motivated and loved. I had this strong knowing that everything was going to be OK and that life was a wondrous thing. I remember feeling overwhelmed with happiness as a beautiful, warm feeling flooded over me. Finally, I felt healed, happy and at peace. I knew Archangel Raziel and the other angels had healed me whilst I was sleeping. I just wanted to jump for joy that hope was alive and in full swing in my heart again. For this healing I was truly grateful. In the next year, I finally found the courage to face the fear of being alone and left my unhappy relationship. At first, every day was a struggle and I prayed all the time, but eventually it got easier, and I was so relieved with my decision. I have never looked back!

Not only have angels appeared in my life to heal me and ease my mind, but they have also appeared to warn me. In 2007 I moved to Sydney for new opportunities and adventure. By that time, I had come a very long way on my journey, had done a lot of soul searching, spiritual seeking and growing. Life was no longer a dreary world but a wondrous world of magic and possibility. I'm not saying that life was perfect, but it was perfect even with all its imperfections. The happiness and joy I felt in my heart was lasting and genuine.

Ever since I began nurturing my passion for crystals I became aware that I was dreaming about crystals quite often, and that these dreams held profound messages. I always pay very close attention to any dreams that have a crystal in them and take extra notice of any messages that they are bringing to me.

One night I had the crystal dream of all crystal dreams! I remember that I was traveling in a car towards my old home and I asked the driver of the car to stop because I had seen some crystals on the side of the road. I ran to the beautiful crystals and realized that they were everywhere, growing along the road. I decided to follow the dirt road and it led to an extremely big shop (I thought at first anyway). But on looking closely, I knew I was graced to be in a truly magical and sacred place. Crystals lined this huge room in every direction. It was so magnificent it took my breath away! I intuitively knew that I was in the presence of the Akashic Records.

Even though I had previously learned that the Akashic Records was a place that recorded all the information of all that ever was, all that is and all that ever will be, it was usually referred to as a gigantic library of books. However, knowing that crystals store ancient information and hold ageless wisdom, I knew that I had truly found myself in the Akashic Records. It was at this moment that a woman walked up to me. At first she appeared like another ordinary human being, with a very nurturing vibration.

She approached me and said "I am here to tell you that very soon a person will enter into your life that you will have the choice of having a relationship with. I am also here to tell you that this person will abuse you and that it is in your highest good to not go down the road of having a relationship with this person." I looked closely at this woman and the loving energy that was vibrating from her and saw that she was an angel in disguise. Love, wisdom and peace were vibrating from her aura. I felt protected, loved and special in her presence. I said to the angel "but can't I just leave the relationship when and if it becomes abusive?" The woman smiled caringly at me and said "No . . . You will not leave because it will be too late. You will have fallen in love!" I remember awakening, feeling very overwhelmed by this strong message of warning. I believe that this angel brought this powerful message to me in a way that she knew I would listen. She must have known that I always listen and pay strong attention to my crystal dreams and take them very seriously.

Not a month had gone by when I did meet someone. I made the decision to go ahead with this relationship with my own free will, telling myself that this might be a different relationship to the one the angel had been speaking of. However, the relationship turned into an extremely abusive one. I had become comfortable with having someone in my life again and found it hard to leave. This made me very angry because I could see that it was most definitely in my highest good to leave, but I felt stuck and afraid. After five months and a much deteriorated self esteem, I left. At first I was devastated by the consequences of the choice I had made. But being very sure now of what I wanted, I bounced back very quickly, with strong determination. Relief settled into my heart, knowing that this experience had come to an end.

The biggest challenge was forgiving myself, especially because it was a mistake I had made before – staying in a situation that wasn't for my highest good. I had promised myself that I would never repeat that mistake, and here I was doing it all over again! So, though after leaving I didn't look back . . . . Truly forgiving myself was another story, and one that I knew would take some time.

The next part of my journey was truly healing. I went on a wondrous holiday to the Hawaiian Islands for five weeks. I traveled to Hawaii with my mother and our friend to participate in Doreen Virtue's Angel Intuitive Advanced course. Both the course and Hawaii were amazing! I was able to slow down and connect with my soul again, to really relax, pamper and care for myself. So by the time I started Doreen Virtue's course I was more than ready for big things to happen. We participated in a Sacred Ceremony one evening called the *makaheki*. This is a ritual to bring what you want into your life. Before I entered the ceremony I searched my heart to the depths and wrote down in my journal what I wished for. I said that I wanted my heart to heal and for it to stop feeling heavy. I wanted to feel joy, lightness and laughter in my heart once again.

We all sat quietly with our intention in mind. Many angels came to us in this amazing ceremony and two in particular were with me. The first was Archangel Raphael. As he approached me I was enveloped by strong emotions of love, peace and a feeling of coming home. In my third eye I saw a little door appear in front of my heart area. Raphael opened this door and healed my heart by infusing it with loving green energy. Raphael then said to me "Stop saying that your heart is heavy; it is making it more so." This meant so much to me as when I really thought about it, I had been saying this a lot and affirming it to the universe and to myself on a constant basis. Raphael then used a beautiful spiritual sword which he swept gently yet firmly across my head to heal any of my thoughts that were not for my highest good.

The second angel I remember clearly was Archangel Uriel. Uriel appeared during the ceremony whilst I was in a deeply meditative state. This might be an important time to mention that nearly 99% of the time I fall asleep during meditations. Uriel took me into a large magnificent building. I remember feeling as though I was protected, loved and in very safe hands. As we walked along a long hall, I noticed that the walls were lined with pictures of people. As I looked closely, I realized that these were women that I had admired greatly throughout my life. Some were friends, some teachers and others were family members, but as I walked along, I was in awe to see all the people who inspired me. It was at this stage that I nearly fell into a deep sleep.

I Remember Uriel saying "You need to stay awake; you need to see this." I forced myself to stay aware and as I reached the end of the hall, I looked at the last picture on the wall. It was a framed picture . . . of me! Uriel said, "It is now time for you to admire yourself and stand in your own power." It was such a moving moment, one I will never forget. So it was in Hawaii that I reconnected with the beauty and love that lives within me. The resentment that I had been holding towards myself simply melted away like the lava flowing from the Hawaiian volcanoes. I know that this beauty has and will always be there. What I attained within myself whilst journeying through Hawaii is something special that will live in my heart forever.

There is one thing I know for sure and that is that the angels have been there for me whenever I have asked, whether it was to help me to see something though their loving eyes, or to soothe me, warn me or heal me. Without a doubt, they have always been there and I am very grateful for all of their support. Now I look forward to a future that I know they are a part of 100%, every step of the way. So thank you for your support angels; thank you for loving me unconditionally. Thank you for always being there for me and for always giving me exactly what I need, and for making the journey oh so much brighter!

It turns out that getting to know the person I am, looking in the mirror and facing my deepest fears was one of the best things I could ever have done. I'm so glad I stopped running from myself and met this challenge head on. My own company, which was something I once feared, is now something I find enjoyable, fun and enriching. I now know that I am capable of achieving more than I ever had dreamed. Sometimes I think that deep down, I always knew that I would grow in genuine confidence and that I would learn to process things that had hurt me, face my fears and that I would learn to embrace who I was . . . and fly! I am reminded of Marianne Williamson's poem *Our Deepest Fear* which refers to our light not our darkness, which frightens us the most. I think that it was my potential that scared me the most. It is not always easy to be brave enough to follow your inner guidance and listen to the unique messages of your inner heart and wisdom and go for your dreams. I know that I couldn't have made it without the angelic support which was with me 100% of the way. I remember the times I felt so lost and alone . . . Deep down in my heart I knew the angels were there with me, holding me in their loving embraces, and that they will continue to do so for all eternity. Not only do they support me though hard times, but they fly next to me whilst I am soaring though the skies, and for this I will always be grateful.

Angelic Dreaming Techniques

Do you find it hard sometimes to hear what your angels are saying? Do you sometimes feel that you are only imagining your answers from them, or feel confused by their information and at a standstill? Then the following techniques are wonderful tools to not only help you to receive those answers you are seeking, but also to help heal and revitalize your body, mind and spirit.

You can try the following techniques just before you go to bed, but the angels also want you to know that anytime is great!

- Have a bath filled with your favorite oils and sea salts, to cleanse your body mind and spirit.

- Make sure your room is a clean space that you love to be in.

- Get a bowl filled with purified water. Hold a glass marble or crystal and imagine all your concerns going into this marble. Say them out loud and send them into the marble. You can also imagine your concerns going in as colours or energy that you no longer desire. When finished, say "I now release all these concerns to my angels before I lay my head down to sleep." Place the marble into the purified water and let it go. The angels will cleanse the water, the marble and as a result, clear your concerns and surround them with love. You are now a clear channel for the angels to come to, to give their guidance and healing.

- Buy and dedicate a plant as your symbolic Angel Plant. Use it as a symbol of your love for them when communicating with your angels.

- Place a picture of an angel or angels above your head where you sleep.

- Obtain a special Angel Journal to write down the questions you want to ask your angels, as well as to record the symbols and responses that you receive. Write letters to your angels in this journal as another way of communicating with them.

- Use a special Angelic Throw Rug dedicated to use while sleeping. This symbolizes the angels being with you always, protecting you as you sleep, and helping you to let go of any concerns or fears you may have. It is basically an all-encompassing cocoon of love to wrap around you while doing this ritual.

- Place a clear quartz crystal under your pillow. This will help your vision to be clear and will heighten the vibration and energy around your question. Visualize your question, write it down or verbally say it out loud whilst holding the crystal. Now, when you lay down to sleep in your sacred space I want you to say the following to your angels: "Angels of love and light, I come to you to ask for your help and guidance upon my sacred journey. From my heart I have a question I need your assistance with. I want to ask this _____. I ask you now for your help upon this matter and I humbly request that you come into my dreams and help me find the key to my question. I ask that you please help me to remember what I need to know from my dream so I can call upon this information in my waking consciousness." It may not always be a question. It may be a request for help or healing. You may ask for help in any way you wish, but always be clear. Remember to always thank your beautiful angels and to show your gratitude. They give so much love to us unconditionally and the one precious gift we can give back to them is gratitude.

• It's a wonderful idea to have a special Angel Candle in whatever colour you feel drawn to. Before you conduct your ritual with your candle, take a moment to anoint it with lavender or any oil of your choice, and then dedicate the candle to the purpose for which you wish to use it. For example, "I dedicate this candle to assist me when I am communicating with the angels before I sleep. Every time I light this candle I am immediately inviting my angels to come to me in my sleep. Whilst I communicate with them, my room is filled with angels and angelic love."

The beauty of asking for angelic guidance is that you can let go of the outcome and really receive their loving help. Sometimes when asking with our conscious mind it can be hard to trust or to really listen, but the angels are happy and willing to help us in any way they can. They would love to help us during sleep time because with our permission, they can really come to us and offer assistance and healing.

Before going to bed, say to your angels "As I sleep, I give all my worries up to you, as you hold my heart and soul in your warm, loving and healing embrace."

Sweet dreams!

Joy

*Your angels say that joy is the
highest expression of your soul.*

*Notice that when you focus on the
joyful aspects of life, these areas grow
and flourish. The angels urge you to
celebrate being alive, to kick off your
shoes and have fun! By expressing joy
through your heart and soul,
you uplift everyone and everything
in your world.*

CLAIRE JENNINGS
Maryborough, Victoria, Australia

CLAIRE JENNINGS has worked with the angels and Archangel Michael in particular since she was a teenager. She became an Angel Intuitive™, certified by Dr Doreen Virtue in 2007.

With her deep love for the angels as well as the elemental and crystal realms, Claire is currently living her dream. She works from home where she gives angel readings and Reiki treatments. Claire also manages an online store selling crystals and soy wax candles which she makes by hand. She finds candle making both a meditative and deeply restorative practice and feels extremely fortunate that such a happy pastime is her "work."

Claire Jennings resides in Victoria, Australia with her amazing husband, two wonderful sons and their dogs.

You may contact Claire through her website: www.EnchantedCupboard.com.au

Archangel Michael –
Protection and Transmutation

CLAIRE JENNINGS

Archangel Michael urges us to laugh, have fun and allow joy into our hearts.
The more joy we pour into our heart, the less room there is for sorrow.

I absolutely adore Archangel Michael and talk to him every single day. I asked him many years ago to live with me and my family and I can't imagine life without him. About three years ago, so that I could have a constant reminder of Archangel Michael's presence, I asked my friend Swati (a very special Angel Therapy Practitioner who shares my passion for this wonderful angel) to make me a silver ring with the words 'Archangel Michael' engraved on it. I have barely removed it since. Even during surgery two years ago, I asked the hospital staff to tape my finger up so I could keep the ring on. I wear it 24 hours a day and just glancing at the ring can be enough to help me through a difficult situation. I love having such a constant *tangible* reminder of his presence, and were I ever brave enough to get a tattoo, it would be an image of Archangel Michael on my side – to represent how he has literally been by my side whenever I have needed him.

He is such a versatile presence, having helped me with everything from writing these very words, giving me courage when I felt fearful, calming my nerves before public speaking, guiding me with business decisions, protecting my family and myself from harm, helping me heal painful relationships and the bruises I carried on my heart, to helping me with electrical appliances, getting my computer to unfreeze and calming me down when I was almost hysterical driving alone in the middle of a very busy city, lost and without a map.

It was Archangel Michael who was there assuring me and comforting me when my second newborn son lay struggling for breath in an incubator. He sat with me up front in the ambulance when we were transferred to a larger city hospital whilst simultaneously watching over my son and the pediatricians who staff the wonderful Neonatal Emergency Transport Service (NETS). He was also there during a most horrendous time in my life on one terribly dark day when I felt hopeless and wretched, and never more ready to give up. He sent me a remarkable sign to urge me *not* to give up, on myself or on life, because I was truly protected and being taken care of. He changed my life and helped me to turn it around, never to be the same again.

I could fill this entire chapter alone detailing the instances that this wonderful angel Michael, whose name means 'He who is like God' has assisted me and my family. But suffice to say he has been an amazing presence and healing force for whom I will be eternally grateful. Although there are not many things we can know for sure on this earth, I *do* know for sure that I will be calling on this mighty archangel until my last day on this planet. I earnestly invite you to ask all the angels, as well as Archangel Michael, into your life if you haven't already. They can be with everyone who needs them simultaneously and they delight in assisting us.

I have been working with Archangel Michael for about 12 years now. In my own personal experience as an Angel Intuitive, regardless of why my client is having a reading, Archangel Michael has consistently made his presence known – either through the actual images on oracle cards when I use them, or I will clairvoyantly see or feel his presence with my client. Whilst I know that Archangel Michael, like all angels, is not restricted by our third dimensional beliefs about time and space and can in fact be in many places simultaneously, I have found myself wondering whether my love for this angel and the fact that he is always with *me* makes me believe that this is so. Or could he really be standing next to every single person I had ever done a reading for? I believe the answer is yes, he is.

There are so many angels and other heavenly helpers that we can call on whenever we need to, but I believe that Archangel Michael is always there whether you are aware of him or not. Regardless of denomination, religious texts around the world all assure us that God (or however you choose to name All that Is) is constantly watching, protecting, and loving us unconditionally. God does this by giving us Archangel Michael who is in God's service. And as God is omnipresent, meaning God is everywhere and part of everything, then so too is Archangel Michael. To borrow from car sales parlance, you could say that Archangel Michael comes 'standard!'

Take a moment to digest that morsel of information. For every step you ever take, you are accompanied by the strongest, most powerful, most courageous, incredibly loving angel there is! Imagine you had an enormous powerfully-built body guard. How safe would you feel walking down the street accompanied by a person of such visible strength? Now imagine this feeling multiplied by an infinite number of times to get an idea of how it feels to have Archangel Michael actively in your life. It's an exciting thought isn't it? He's watching out for you and protecting you. You have an infinite supply of assistance with you always, just waiting to be requested.

And there lies the key. Archangel Michael may be walking with each and every one of us, but he cannot step in and help us unless we ask him to. Why can't he just barge in when required and save the day? Because we all have the gift of free will, and the angels will never interfere with or try to override a person's free will. With the exception of intervening should our life be threatened before our time, the angels will stand back on the sidelines, giving you nudges when necessary, but it is up to us to follow these nudges. It cannot be forced upon us. If it could, it would defeat the whole point of coming here and having this earthly experience. We come here to learn and to grow and we cannot grow spiritually by being spoon fed. The angels cannot and will not do that. What they can do however is provide us with a multitude of tools that we can use in our day to day lives to help us grow, to keep us safe and to assist us with even the most ordinary events in our daily life, including all the challenges and highlights.

My personal toolbox includes healing techniques from Archangel Raphael, and de-cluttering and beautification tips from Archangel Jophiel. While Archangel Ariel helps me with my finances, Archangel Raziel assists me on my spiritual journey and with accessing Higher Knowledge. And I call upon Archangel Metatron daily to help me parent and take care of my children, and then again in the evening, to stand along side Archangel Michael and watch over my family whilst they sleep. The list is potentially endless and I encourage you to learn more about each Archangel that interests you. A great place to start learning about Archangels and the areas in which they can assist you is the book *Archangels and Ascended Masters*, as well as the *Archangel Oracle Cards,* both written by my teacher Doreen Virtue and published by Hay House. As well as being one of my most influential teachers to date, Doreen is an internationally recognized expert on angels and has so far written about fifteen of the Archangels. There are potentially many more yet to be identified to us as well, and these Archangels will come into our consciousness as we need them, and as we ascend into Higher Consciousness and become more able to connect with them.

Whilst I use these tools outlined above on a daily basis, I would particularly like to share and focus on some tools I have learned from Archangel Michael that we can use to protect us and assist us in releasing old energy that no longer serves us.

Archangel Michael has been insisting lately on the importance of transmutation. For those who are not familiar with this term, to transmute something is to take one thing and turn it into something else completely. For example: the transformation of negative energy into positive energy. He says that whilst shielding and

> ### Archangel Michael
>
> *You are safe, as the Archangel of protection is with you right now.*
>
> *Archangel Michael reminds us that there is no power greater than God's love. Allow him to fill you with courage to face any fears or challenges in your life, knowing that you are completely safe and secure.*

cord cutting are great, it's time to take it to the next level. As Lightworkers, one of our roles is to bring more positivity into the world, or to look at it another way, to reduce negativity! How do we do this? Just protecting ourselves is no longer enough – let's think about how to *reduce* that negative energy.

For example, say we are feeling bombarded by a negative person or perhaps we are even the subject of their angry thoughts, feelings or actions. We could most certainly shield ourselves from this negativity by surrounding ourselves with a bubble of light, and perhaps set the intention that it will bounce back to the person sending us those unpleasant vibes, or use energetic mirrors to reflect the energy back. However, as a result of this shielding, you might have the unpleasant surprise of feeling even *more* bombarded by this person or feeling as if they are 'amping up' their attack on you. Have you ever experienced that?

By doing this, we have certainly protected ourselves in the first instance, but how have we done so? By *sending* the negativity right back! Yes that's right! You've just unwittingly thrown down the challenge to create more conflict! That is why I have had clients who have come to me very distressed, because the more they have shielded and protected themselves from a situation, the worse it has become. They have not realized that they are taking that negative energy and are flinging it right back at the person who flung it at them! The original 'thrower' feels most upset to feel this negative energy come flying back at them. As far as they are concerned you have just declared war! Goodness, isn't it getting complicated?! Let's make it simpler.

If by shielding you are bouncing negativity straight back to the source, what is the alternative? It's better to ask Archangel Michael to transmute that energy to Love before it is returned! As human beings we can struggle to send love to someone who is perhaps behaving less than ideally towards us, but with this method we don't have to. We simply ask Archangel Michael to protect us throughout our day, and ask that if any negativity is sent towards us this day that it be returned to the person who sent it, after being transmuted to Light energy, or in other words, to Divine Love. Give it a try! I feel sure you will be amazed at the difference! By taking the time to ask for the energy to be transmuted, you are not only helping yourself and the other person involved – you are helping the planet, one interaction at a time.

If Love is to prevail, it stands to reason that there has to be *more* of it, don't you think? By simply pushing the negativity away or back to the sender it remains out there, just swirling around getting pushed from place to place. Let's remove it altogether and replace it with Divine Love! And that is what working at the 'front line' or what 'making the world a better place' is all about. You can't achieve anything in life simply floating along wrapped up in a bubble! Archangel Michael urges us to take it one step further. I can think of a dozen examples of how to utilize this tool in my daily life. Try seeing how many you can come up with too! Here are just a few to get you started.

- You go shopping at the store and a cashier is hostile and unfriendly. You can a) deflect that energy straight back to him/her, the result being that they feel even worse OR b) you can set the intention before you go shopping that any negativity sent your way be returned *after* being transmuted to Love, and the cashier will most likely feel a little better without knowing why. It may be too late for *you* to benefit from this shift in energy during this transaction but I guarantee you will have put something very worthwhile in motion which you can feel good about!

Other examples include:

- A family member giving you a hard time at a family function

- Dealing with an uncooperative tradesperson

- When *you* are the cashier or other public service person and are feeling the ire from people waiting in queues with complaints, etc.

- Going into a meeting at work or in your community where the energy feels negative or you know it will be filled with potentially negative people

Try this for yourself. I am sure you will be amazed at the results!

Now that we have talked a little about protection with Archangel Michael, I would like to talk a little about releasing with Archangel Michael. One of the things I love the most about this wonderful angel is how incredibly diverse he is! He can protect us, release us from fear, listen to all our troubles whenever we need an empathetic ear, and he can help us release what no longer serves us in our life missions here on Earth. We all have things that we are hanging on to, but which do not serve us. I am mainly talking about emotions here, although clutter and excessive 'stuff' can really get in the way of the path forward for many people. If you are currently struggling with physical clutter, I recommend a little chat with Archangel Jophiel. She is the most amazing de-clutter expert around and will be glad to be of assistance to you. (Remember, if you want her assistance you have to ask first!)

If I could emphasize just one thing, it would be the importance of what I call Spiritual Hygiene. It's right up there with flossing and taking a shower! Every day we collect experiences, emotions, thoughts and energy. Of course some of this is very good. Some of it is not. Negative self talk, family issues, stressful days at work, sharp words – all translate into negative energy surrounding and permeating your aura and Spiritual body every day. I see this energy clairvoyantly as a dark sticky stain. To illustrate, imagine you are making breakfast and whilst making your toast, you drop a blob of jam or honey or something equally sticky on the floor and you just leave it there. Someone comes along and stands in it and gets sock fluff in it. You flick all the crumbs off the bench onto the floor instead of cleaning up and they land in the sticky mess.

As the day goes by, the gooey mess gets dirtier and dirtier and you have this weird sticky yet fluffy black mark on the floor gathering and attracting more and more dirt. You don't clean it off for several weeks. It's dried out when you finally get around to cleaning it off and it sure takes some scrubbing! Now rewind the scenario and imagine that you drop the jam or honey on the floor and you grab some paper towel and wipe it off straight away. Its quick, it's easy and you will forget it ever happened very quickly. It was dealt with quickly so it left no lasting damage.

Can you see how we can relate that to our emotional baggage? Anger, grief, pain – the whole gamut of negative emotion – is the jam. We can either pretend it's not there and let it gather a whole ton of additional gunk on it until it makes a dreadful stain which is difficult to get off (dis-ease), OR we can quickly and easily remove it on a daily basis so it leaves no lasting or damaging marks. What would you rather do? I know what I would prefer, and that's why at the end of each day I hand all my 'jam spots' to Archangel Michael. I place them all in his very groovy 'Magical Transmutational Basket.'

At the end of each day I spend some time thinking about my day and what experiences I've had and note whether they were good, bad or indifferent. I give a few words of gratitude for the good and throw away the rest! I visualize plucking each negative item from my aura and handing it to Archangel Michael. He stands next to me smiling, holding his magical basket which is filled with luminescent fluid that shimmers as I drop each item into it. The fluid is pink and violet with swirls of white and gold. It is Magical Transmutational Liquid of course! As each item is dropped into the basket it mysteriously vanishes, having been transmuted into positive and loving energy.

I drop in everything I can think of and then scan my body with my mind's eye to look for anything else I can release. This is where I can release things that have happened a long time ago, before I knew about angels who carry funky baskets! After I have finished dropping everything I wish into the basket, I ask that all the empty spaces I have created by removing all my 'jam spots' be filled with Divine White Light. There is no such thing as a vacuum. When you remove something, you need to replace it with something else. Something much better! I give thanks to Archangel Michael for his precious gift and happily go to bed feeling unburdened and peaceful. This basket is a great place to put all your worry too!

Worry is negative prayer and goes out to the Universe to be heard just the same as positive prayer! Dumping it into our basket is a safe way of pouring out all our worries and concerns, as we can be assured those concerns will be carried safely away. We all have worry at one time or another, which I see as little termite-like creatures burrowing into our peaceful vibration and eating through it. It's never the emotion that causes problems – only how we deal with it! Always be assured that you can pour your heart out to the angels. If you've been holding back for whatever reason, give it a try and feel how much lighter your heart becomes. The best thing about the Magical Transmutational Basket is that it is much like Mary Poppin's carpet bag – never ending. No matter what your sorrows, you could never ever overfill it. It is infinite in its ability to receive what you place into it. Such are the blessings we can receive from the angels.

At the end of this chapter I will take you through this process in more detail so you can feel confident in your ability to utilize this releasing tool. As I said earlier, we come here to learn and absorb what we can from this earthly experience. I feel we also need to learn discernment too! There is no need to hang on to every last thing we hear, feel, say and experience. It does not serve us; indeed it only serves to hinder us. Learning to perfect the old adage of "keep the baby but throw out the bath water" is one of the most valuable Earth lessons we can learn during our time here.

Finally, Archangel Michael would like all of us to know that as always, the best defense is to have a good offence! You have likely heard the old cliché that laughter is the best medicine? Well it's true! The best protection against negativity and fear based living is to live joyously! Archangel Michael urges us to laugh, have fun and allow joy into our hearts. The more joy we pour into our heart, the less room there is for sorrow. There cannot be dark where there is light. Frances Hodgson Burnett sums it up in my favorite childhood book *The Secret Garden*, when she writes of Dicken and his mother talking in their cottage garden about the importance of filling Colin's life with good if he is to get well. She explains to Dicken that "Wherever thou tend a rose my lad, a thistle cannot grow." You are a beautiful rose, blooming in God's garden, being tended to by the most loving gardeners imaginable – the angels. And it's your time to reach to the sky, in full spectacular bloom as the very loved, completely protected, always provided for, precious Child of God that you are.

How to Use the Magical Transmutational Basket

This is best done at the end of the day, whilst taking a sea salt bath or sitting or lying quietly in bed, if you can be sure you won't fall asleep half way through! Next, call on Archangel Michael and ask him to sit with you whilst you put all of your cares into his basket. I would like to emphasize the importance of *you* placing the items in the basket. Whilst you can certainly ask Archangel Michael to place them in the basket for you and he will do so, he also emphasizes the importance of *empowerment*. These are your feelings after all – take charge of them! Take responsibility for them and make the decision to transmute them forever yourself, with Archangel Michael standing by, supporting you every step of the way. You may think there's little difference, but it is incredibly empowering to own your own 'stuff' – even stuff you want to get rid of.

Once you have called in Archangel Michael you may feel his presence as a warm energy. You may see him as an angel or as purple light. You may hear his voice. You may experience nothing at all. If this is the case, rest assured that he is most certainly still with you holding the basket! Pay attention to what the basket looks like. Form an impression of what it might look like in your mind if you don't get an actual image. This is important, as you are more likely to use the basket if it is personal, familiar and comfortable for you. For example, my basket is white wicker with pink gingham lining because I like that style. However, if pink gingham gives you nightmares because you were made to wear it constantly as a child or if your taste is very contemporary and un-gingham-like, then you will not feel comfortable with this process and you are less likely to use it.

Now that you have settled on a basket style, start to think about the day you've just had. There is no need to start dredging up every negative emotion you've ever had all at once – let's start with the present moment. Firstly, think of all the good things that happened to you today. Give thanks to your angels for walking with you, and show gratitude to the Universe for everything good. Now think about anything negative that happened or anything that made you feel angry or upset. Imagine where these things, which are shaped like black blobs or dots, are sitting in your body. Scan over your body in your mind's eye if an area doesn't come immediately to mind. If you still can't find anything, ask Archangel Michael to assist. The first thing that pops into your mind after asking for assistance will be the place to start. This is your body; these are your feelings and you are guided every step of the way by your angel team, so you don't need to worry about making a mistake – it's impossible!

See yourself lifting away that negative feeling or experience and dropping it into your basket. See it dissolve into the liquid, forever transmuted. Continue to drop in everything negative from that day that you wish to release. After you have finished, you may wish to continue into the past. You might find that releasing something that happened today has brought up something which happened last week. Keep going until you feel you have done enough for today. Ask Archangel Michael if you are not sure. Resist the temptation to try to clear away every bad feeling you've ever had in one sitting. You will exhaust yourself and you can end up feeling completely drained and emotionally overwhelmed, which is the exact opposite of how we are aiming to feel! You can always release a little more tomorrow.

Ask for your body to be filled with Divine White Light. Bask in this wonderful feeling for a moment. When you are ready, give thanks to Archangel Michael for protecting you and overseeing this beautiful process. Then enjoy the rest of your evening and a restful night's sleep!

Peace

*Your angels want you to know
that all is well in your universe.*

*Know that you will always be loved
and provided for, and that everything
is flowing in your life exactly as it
should. Your sense of inner peace
increases the more you express
gratitude and appreciation, and allow
the angels to lovingly support you
whenever you need help.*

MARYELLEN DE VINE
Los Gatos, California USA

MARYELLEN DE VINE is a spiritual teacher and intuitive who brings joy as well as the sacred to all her workshops, ceremonies, and events. She teaches in-person, on-line, and tele-workshops, which are perfectly suited for the beginner and the advanced student. She loves assisting and empowering others as they step along their spiritual path. Maryellen is a certified Angel Therapy Practitioner® certified by Doreen Virtue PhD, a Reiki Master, a licensed minister, and has studied many spiritual and healing modalities.

Known as compassionate and Light-filled, Maryellen approaches her work to inspire, uplift and empower. She facilitates beautiful sacred ceremonies and meditation journeys, and creates flower, crystal, and angel/ascended master essences and aura sprays. She is the proud mother of three beautiful boys, and lives with her husband and sons in Northern California. Being a wife, mother and Angel Therapy Practitioner®, Maryellen knows how difficult it can be to find balance in our busy lives. She enjoys assisting others in finding harmony in all areas of their lives by using spiritual tools.

If you are interested in her classes, services, or products, please visit her website at www.AngelicJourneys.com.

Everyday Sacred Ceremony with the Angels

MARYELLEN DE VINE

*For those of us who would like to bring a greater sense
of sacred connection to our everyday life,
ceremony is a wonderful way to bridge Heaven and Earth.*

Angels are an important part of my life. They guide me, comfort me, and assist me. They remind me that I am not alone on this path called life. One of the ways I love asking the angels to assist me and bless me is through sacred ceremony. Through the physical act of ceremony, we are telling God and the angels that we choose to participate in the manifestation of our dreams and desires. We are taking action, even if it only seems like symbolic acts.

The angels have shared with me so often the importance of blending Heaven and Earth in our spiritual practice. Many of us spend much of our time looking upwards for our spiritual assistance. Yet we often forget about all that God has given us that is part of life on Earth. We live on Earth, walk upon it, breathe the air, receive food that nourishes us, and have material things to clothe us and give us enjoyment. The things we wish to manifest in our lives are frequently rooted in our three-dimensional existence here on Earth. Even though we are spiritual beings, filled with light, we are blessed with physical bodies and their many senses. We see the beauty of a sunset, smell the delicate fragrance of a flower, feel the warm sun upon our skin, hear the delightful laugh of a baby, and taste the many flavors of our foods. We are also blessed with feeling emotion. We would certainly miss much if we didn't feel joy, love and excitement.

For those of us who would like to bring a greater sense of sacred connection to our everyday life, ceremony is a wonderful way to bridge Heaven and Earth. Sacred ceremony empowers us, and it also honors Mother Earth. Since God created everything and is in everything, everything has spirit, and everything is sacred and holy. In the ancient days, people revered Mother Earth for all that they received from Her. Most people in our modern times take Her for granted. Yet, when we acknowledge the blessings and qualities of the earth, air, fire, and water; when we honor the sacred spirit within the animals, the birds, the trees, and the minerals; we acknowledge what we have been blessed with.

I asked for messages to share with you about sacred ceremony. I sat quietly and connected first with the energy of sacred ceremony itself. Here is the message I received:

Allow me to bless and heal your soul in a way that is different from what you may be used to. I am able to encompass all of creation; all that God has created. From utilizing the mountain's strength to the energy of the gently flowing stream; from the bird's-eye view to the igniting of the fire within your soul; all of this is done with the help of the elements and all that is co-existing with you upon this earth. You create 'sacred community' by working together with all that God has gloriously made for you to live with. Walk hand-in-hand with them as you would your human brothers and sisters, and allow Heaven and Earth to assist you together.

Next I asked the angels to share a message about sacred ceremony:

We are always happy to bring a little ease into your life. When you are struggling with something, and even though it may be an opportunity for growth and healing, we wish to lessen the discomfort for you. We love that you look to us for help and blessings. We wish to acknowledge the wondrous power you have at your fingertips with the actions you take by performing sacred ceremony. By combining prayers with your physical actions, you are empowering yourself. You are not powerless and needing to wait for us to 'help make the situation better for you,' but instead you are, together with us, utilizing that which God has graciously provided. When you wish to see one of your desires come true, through sacred ceremony, you are 'shouting out to the universe' that you are stepping forward in co-creating this desire along with Heaven and Earth. Physical action grounds the wishes that are floating up to Heaven into Earthly reality. We wish for you to feel empowered, to know that you can co-create miracles in your life! We cheer you on as we walk by your side – always!

We are accustomed to sacred ceremony in weddings, baptisms and funerals, yet there are many other types of ceremony that we can perform for our daily living:

- Releasing
- Blessing
- Manifesting
- Healing
- Celebrating
- Transitions
- Milestones
- Endings

For example, if you add sacred ceremony to a birthday celebration, you'll find that it becomes a very memorable event for all involved. Here is a ceremony I facilitated with a group of women to celebrate and honor their dear friend Kelsey's birthday. Her friend Michelle hosted the party at her home on a December evening and cooked a sumptuous meal for her guests. Before the event, each guest received a card with the words "My birthday wish for Kelsey is . . . " printed on top, so she could write a special message. The evening started with a guided meditation in which each guest's angel took her to a private garden. In this garden, they were able to release the year that was ending, and seed their intentions and wishes for the new year ahead.

After the meditation, the group moved to the dining room for dinner. While they were eating, I returned to the original room and lit candles throughout the space. When it was time for everyone to come in, I asked them to enter quietly with the mindset of entering sacred space. It was a beautiful space with flowers and candles around the room. I rang a bell to signify the beginning of the ceremony and lit a candle on the altar, made from a small table with a cloth draped over it. I asked the angels to be present and for the room to be filled with light and love. I explained the items I had on the altar that represented the elements, and some of the qualities each element brings to us:

- For the element of fire, I used the candle and its flame. Fire represents transformation and purification.

- For the element of air, the smoke from the candle would carry our wishes and prayers up to the heavens. Air represents the breath of life, inspiration, and seeing things from a higher perspective.

- The element of water was represented by two items. The first was a cleansing spray I had made with a blend of essential oils specifically for that evening. I misted the air in the room and over each of us. The bottle of spray was then given to the birthday girl as my gift. Also on the altar was some water in a small, clear teapot. Water represents emotions, cleansing and purifying, renewal and rebirth.

- For the element of Earth, there were two things: a pouch of stones and a single rose. Earth represents grounding, stability and strength, ancient wisdom and power.

After the explanations, I took a moment to honor Kelsey's mother, who was also in attendance, for bringing Kelsey into our lives, and handed her the rose. A flowering jasmine tea ball was put into the clear teapot of water, representing the blossoming of the group's friendship. I asked the ladies to place their left hand on their heart and to extend their right hand toward the teapot. They were to visualize their heart energy flowing through their arm and into the teapot, while I spoke a blessing over the tea. I poured small amounts of the tea into little cartoon cups (representing Kelsey's playful side) and passed them around. As everyone drank the tea, they physically took in both the blessings of the group and one another's heart energy.

One by one, each person then came up to Kelsey, read their card to her, and placed it in a special keepsake box. I followed up with a card I wrote with a message from her angels. Kelsey was handed the pouch of stones that were engraved with words. She stood in front of each person, picked out a stone, held it to her heart to fill it with her love and gratitude, and then handed it to the person.

We then stood in a circle, holding hands, while a beautiful song about birthdays played. Then we played a happy, 'rocking out' birthday song. I closed the ceremony by thanking the ladies and the angels for participating in this joyous occasion, ringing the bell, and blowing out the candle.

This is what Michelle wrote about the event afterwards:

Finding a way to honor a friend on her birthday can be as simple as making reservations and calling a few friends. However, if you want to make a lasting impression, then a birthday ceremony is the way to go. It is a celebration filled with love and gratitude worthy of a special friend. The evening turned out to be one of the most memorable, personable, and intimate celebrations I have ever witnessed. There is none more deserving than a person whose friendship is cherished by so many. We all have them in our lives and now we have a way to show them how truly cherished they are!

I've enjoyed doing many different kinds of ceremony. Some have been performed alone and some with others. The ones that I conduct most often for myself are releasing ceremonies, blessing ceremonies, and manifesting ceremonies. I recognize the need to do a releasing ceremony when I'm feeling blocked or stuck, have fears coming to the surface, or just need to release feelings of overwhelm with all that is on my plate. It is amazing how different I feel after doing a releasing ceremony! Sometimes I feel lighter, sometimes I feel very tired, and sometimes I feel energized. No matter how I am left feeling, I know that powerful work has been done.

I like to perform ceremonies that bless projects I am working on, such as when I first created my website, when I am working on a writing project, or creating a new workshop. I ask the angels to bless the project and all the people those projects will touch. Blessing ceremonies can be created to bless a new career, a home, a relationship – anything at all!

Manifesting ceremonies can be done independently or combined with releasing ceremonies. After releasing that which we are ready to let go of, we make room within ourselves to allow in what we'd like to bring into our lives. We may choose to focus on one particular thing, such as prosperity, or we may choose to include the many things we desire, such as good health, abundance, loving relationships, a new job, balance in our lives, etc. These types of ceremonies can be done as we face challenges, and when we realize that we are ready to let go of things that no longer serve us. They can also bring blessings to our lives and help us attract the things we desire.

I have also performed ceremonies with my husband and children. When our cat passed away, we performed a ceremony where each of us said a little something in remembrance of him and then mixed some of his ashes into a small amount of dirt to spread in our yard. When my boys were very young, we did a transition ceremony to help them give up their pacifiers. I had them think about what worried them about giving up the pacifiers, and then had them blow those worries into a rock they each picked out for this purpose. (I blew out my fears of having sleepless nights during the transition!)

We usually have a small gathering of family at our house each Christmas Eve. One year I wanted to perform a simple ceremony before we opened presents to honor what Christmas is really about. I gave each person a white candle. I had them come up one by one and I lit their candle with my pink candle. I stated that Christmas is a celebration of the birth of Christ and that we give gifts in honor of this. I said that my pink candle represented unconditional love, because that's what Christ was, and is, all about. After everyone's candles were lit, we listened to the song *O Holy Night*, and I said a closing prayer. And that was it, short and sweet! Everyone commented as they were leaving that night on how nice it was to add this ceremony to our usual celebration.

You can make your own ceremonies simple and quick or elaborate and lengthy. You may add the sacred to your everyday celebrations, such as birthdays, holidays, anniversaries, and baby showers. You can acknowledge milestones, transitions, and endings. It can be a lot of fun thinking of things to put in your ceremony. You may include things that will create warm, loving feelings, a sense of joy and lightness, and the feelings of empowerment, acknowledgment and honoring.

You can also ask your angels to assist you in creating your ceremonies. Notice any ideas that suddenly pop into your head, or thoughts about items that call to you to be included. I have found that when I follow this guidance, the ceremony always has a very powerful surprise element to it. You might feel a strong impulse

> ### Release
>
> *As you let go of the past, you allow new blessings to flow towards you.*
>
> *Your angels ask that you release any aspect of your life that is no longer working. Let go of any struggle and free your heart of all burdens. By surrendering these to your angels, they can be lovingly replaced with new inspiration, opportunities and unexpected blessings.*

to include a particular crystal, your drum might catch your eye, or a greeting card with particularly appropriate words may grab your attention. Just enjoy the creative process, and have fun with it! You may choose to include sound, such as drumming, chanting, or singing; movement, such as dance, yoga, or walking a labyrinth; art, such as making a sacred talisman, creating a collage, or painting/coloring. Music, meditation, energy healing, journaling, and receiving messages from your angels through oracle cards are just some of the many things you can include in your private or group ceremony.

Remember to trust your intuition. You could be in the middle of a ceremony and suddenly get the guidance to do something different from what you had planned, or to add something extra. Go ahead and follow that guidance, as Spirit knows just the right thing for just the right moment. You might also find that you spontaneously do an impromptu ceremony. All ceremony is good! Bringing the sacred into everyday events adds richness to our lives.

Here are a couple examples of my wonderful experiences with ceremony when I listened and acted on my guidance:

I was doing a ceremony to bless a new project I was working on. Halfway through, I suddenly felt the angels wanting me to dance with them. Okay – if the angels want to dance, I'll dance! I had some uplifting harp music playing and I started to flit about the room. As I did, I could really feel them dance with me – it was so wonderful! When we were finished with our dancing, I went back to continue my ceremony, now in an almost euphoric mood. As I proceeded, it felt like my angels had their wings wrapped around me and I could feel their love for me so strongly. Tears of love and gratitude ran down my cheeks as I continued with my now extra-special ceremony.

Another time, while getting ready in the morning, I had received an image of leading a releasing ceremony with some friends at a nearby park. I was seeing them looking for a piece of nature to release into and then finding a place by the park's creek to throw it into. Since I had at that time been feeling blocked and having difficulty with a writing project, I thought I'd go to the park and do that same releasing ceremony. When I got to the appropriate section of the park, I saw that some young trees had been planted in a couple of places. How nice! In one rounded corner of the lawn were planted some young oak trees in a semi-circle. Together with the older trees already around the other side, they now created a circle of trees. What a wonderful place to perform ceremony! I was guided to do a ceremony right then and there to consecrate this as sacred space. I called in the spirits of the directions and the elements and the archangels associated with the directions.

When I faced east for the element of air, the breeze blew mightily; at south for the element of fire, the sun was low and off to the left, and was shining on me and warming me; at west and the element of water, I was facing the creek; at north and the element of Earth, I was facing a large group of trees. I asked God and the angels to bless this space as holy and sacred. A couple of robins came near and one in particular kept hopping closer and closer to the circle. I spoke to the robin and all the other 'winged friends,' asking them to watch over and bless this space. I called to Jesus to walk with me around the circle to bless each young oak tree. When I noticed a mound of dirt made by a mole, I asked him to be the groundskeeper. I also called in the faeries to keep the space light and to watch over it. I whispered to all the beautiful, elder oak trees all around the park to help these young ones to grow into mighty, wise trees. I collected a couple pieces of trash and a squashed drink can to ceremonially place into a trashcan and recycling bin when I would leave the park.

It felt like the perfect time to initiate this sacred ceremonial space with my own releasing ceremony, so I looked around for a piece of nature that would be willing to take on what I wanted to release, and found a small stick. As I stood in the center of the circle, I thought about the blocks I was experiencing and connected to the energy of them. When I felt ready, I walked over to the creek, blew into the stick to relinquish those blocks into the stick, thanked the stick, and then tossed it into a part of the creek that had lots of lush green growth (representing the lush growth of writing I would then be able to do). I was drawn to some acorns on the ground and looked for the right and perfect one to bring home with me as a reminder of this ceremony. The one that called to me had one end broken. I felt this represented that 'broken' part of me: my blocks and fears. I then was drawn to another 'perfect' acorn and picked that one up to represent that I really am whole and perfect. As I was giving thanks to all that assisted, I noticed a white bird flying overhead. This white bird seemed to represent the purification that had just been completed. After closing the circle, I heard a hawk in the sky crying out with delight. What a perfect ending to this ceremony!

Here are some things to consider when creating your ceremonies:

- Your intention for your ceremony – Is it to release, to bless, to celebrate?

- Will you perform your ceremony alone or with others?

- Where will you hold your ceremony? – Will it be spreading a scarf on your bedroom floor, sitting under a tree, or renting a hall?

- Items to include on your altar – It's always nice to include something that represents each of the elements (air, fire, water, earth) and Spirit. You can include a statue of an angel, faerie, ascended master, or animal. Items needed for things that you will be doing in your ceremony can be placed on your altar.

- What will you be doing in your ceremony? – Will you include meditation, journaling or art? How will you be honoring the guest of honor?

I hope this has inspired you to add sacred ceremony to your everyday life. Not only are you adding deeper meaning and spiritual presence to your day-to-day living, you are also honoring and including Mother Earth in your life.

In the following section, you will find instructions for performing a releasing and manifesting ceremony. A common version, which I love, is to find a piece of nature (stick, rock, feather, etc.) that will be used to relinquish that which you are going to release. However, since this is a ceremony that may be familiar to many people, I would like to offer you a variation that you can add to your spiritual toolbox.

Enjoy!

Releasing and Manifesting Ceremony

We often have things in our lives that we are ready to release. We may want to release stress, blocks and fears, unforgiveness, a habit, a health challenge, or an unhealthy relationship. When we release these unwanted things, we make room for our true wishes and desires to come into our lives.

Take some time to sit quietly and get clear on what you are ready to release and what you desire to bring into your life.

When you are ready to perform your ceremony, create your altar. This can be a scarf placed on your bed or on the ground, or it can be on a tabletop or tree stump. Place on your altar items which represent the four elements. If you know the geographic directions in your location, place your items in the corresponding direction as noted below. Also noted are the archangels associated with the directions and elements.

- Feather – Air – East – Archangel Raphael

- Candle – Fire – South – Archangel Michael

- Small bowl of water – Water – West – Archangel Gabriel

- Crystal or rock – Earth – North – Archangel Uriel

Place any other items you'd like, such as a statue of an angel, a representative of what you are releasing and/or what you want to call in to your life.

Other items to have available are:

- Paints (can be as simple as a child's paint set)

- Paintbrushes

- Water for rinsing brushes

- Paper to use as your canvas (multiple sheets)

- Newspaper or plastic sheet to protect surface

- Paper towels

- Paper plates to use for mixing colors

Begin your ceremony by lighting the candle. Facing one direction at a time, hold up your representation of each element, and invite the spirits of that element and direction, and the corresponding archangel to be present to create a sacred circle around you. Ask God to fill your circle with light and ask your angels to assist you with the upcoming process. With your painting supplies ready, connect to what you want to release (really feel it), choose the colors you are drawn to and begin to paint an expression of what's being released. Just let it flow out of you. Don't think about how you think the painting 'should' look. Use a separate sheet of paper for each thing you are releasing. Take as much time as you need to get it out of your body and onto the paper. Visualize Archangel Michael cutting the cord that is connecting you to the thing you're releasing. When finished, take each painting and crumple it up to be thrown away.

Next, connect to what it would feel like to have those things that you wish to bring into your life. Visualize yourself as already having them. Feel how it feels to already have them. Think about how it benefits and blesses you and those around you. Visualize how your having them creates joy in your life and creates a ripple effect on the planet. Now paint those desires and intentions. Choose the colors you are guided to. Let the paintbrush move by itself, expressing the energy and feelings of these desires. Use as many sheets of paper as you wish. Ask your angels and the element of air to send these wishes up with the smoke of the candle to the heavens. Ask Mother Earth to ground these wishes into your life here on Earth. Thank the element of fire for transmuting any negative energy into loving and healing energies. Dip your fingers into the bowl of water, thanking the element of water for cleansing and purifying you.

You will be keeping these paintings as they now are imbued with the powerful energy of this ceremony. Sit quietly and ask your angels for any action steps you can take to assist in bringing forward your desires, or to clear any residue of what was released.

To end the ceremony, face each direction and thank the direction, elements, and archangels for giving their blessings and powerful assistance, and acknowledge the closing of the sacred circle.

∽

Blessing

We wish you many blessings as you listen for the whispers of the angels . . .

May Archangel Michael
always be at your right hand,
Archangel Gabriel at your left,
Archangel Uriel before you,
Archangel Raphael behind you,
the Holy Spirit above your head,
the Sacred Earth beneath your feet.
May peace be with you, always.

New Beginnings

*Your angels invite you to embrace
a new cycle in your life.*

*Change is a blessing. Breathe in
deeply all that is New! Celebrate this
shedding of an old skin. Give thanks
for the multitude of gifts arriving in
your life. Feel yourself freed from the
cocoon of old ways. You are now ready
to spread your wings and fly!*

Acknowledgements

Immense gratitude goes to all of the remarkable Angel Experts who've shared their heartfelt wisdom and professional expertise throughout the pages of this book. Your loving dedication to working with your clients and the angelic realm is truly inspirational!

Many thanks to Wendy Gabriel whose original vision it was to create this book, and to Fiona Raven for her assistance in crafting its magical pages. We also wish to thank the authors' friends and families for supporting them on this journey. Finally, thank you to Archangel Gabriel for guiding the birth of this book with so much love.

About Soul Wings® Press

Publishing for the Soul®

Soul Wings® Press is an award-winning Small Press Publisher.
We specialize in providing compassionate, professional editorial services
and quality book publishing to assist experts in the fields of
Self-help and Spirituality to become published authors.

If you wish to read interviews with our authors,
or become an author yourself, please visit our website.
www.SoulWingsPress.com

Soul Wings Press® Titles
of related Interest

Soul Whispers: Collective Wisdom from Soul Coaches around the World 2009
Soul Whispers II: Secret Alchemy of the Elements in Soul Coaching 2011
Planet Whispers: Wisdom from Soul Travelers around the World 2011

www.ingramcontent.com/pod-product-compliance
Lightning Source LLC
Chambersburg PA
CBHW071443090426
42737CB00011B/1757